# THE PERFORMER
# PREPARES

# The Performer Prepares

# Robert Caldwell

Pst...Inc

Dallas

Copyright 1990 by Pst...Inc
All rights reserved
No part of this book may be reproduced in any form without
permission in writing from the publisher.
Published by Pst...Inc
P.O. Box 800208C
Dallas, Texas 75380
cover design Carla Johnson
edited by Diane Dupuis
Library of Congress Catalogue Card Number: 89-64407

First Edition

1 2 3 4 5 6 7 8 9 10

ISBN: 1-877761- 26-5 SB

*to Joan*

# CONTENTS

# ACKNOWLEDGMENTS

The approach in this book is based on the contributions of so many people that I will simply list them: Janet Bookspan, Lili Kraus, Dr. Milton Erickson, Dr. John Grinder, Dr. Richard Bandler, Steve and Connie Rae Andreas, Dr. Herbert Benson, Wallace Stevens, Dr. Victor Frankl, Gregory Bateson, Leslie Cameron Bandler, Genie Labourde, Paul Tillich, Rollo May, Charlie Schneider, Beverly Stoy, Edgar Davis. Each of their stimulating and often provocative ideas, insights, and techniques echo through these pages.

I am especially grateful for my three years of weekly performance classes with Joan Wall, where many new techniques were tried, tested, and refined. Her unending support and encouragement has been deeply appreciated.

Without Alice Walker, whose friendship, eagerness, and meteoric improvements in performance in the early days, my interest may never have taken such a foothold.

Finally, my deepest thanks and love to my wife Bobbie, without whose complete involvement from start to finish, this book simply would not have been possible.

# I NTRODUCTION

Several years ago, as I was exploring more effective approaches to performing, I happened to hear a recital by mezzo Joan Wall during which her presence expanded radiantly from the stage and enveloped the audience. The depth, subtlety, and richness of the music that streamed into the hall epitomized the very qualities I was searching for.

I spoke with her later about her performing and discovered that she had always been comfortable performing, from childhood through her career at the Metropolitan Opera, in Europe, and even now, during her occasional concerts. I wanted to know all about it. How did she prepare? What was her attitude? Why didn't she get an attack of nerves like some other performers? Why didn't she buckle when singing in front of a great conductor? Why didn't the audience distract her? And so on.

She assured me that underneath her apparent ease she worked quite hard. She explained that after she thoroughly memorizes the music and strategically solves the technical problems, then, more or less, her performance work begins. First she forms an image of the whole perfor-

What, specifically, is different about powerful performers?

mance. Then, in her rehearsal work, Joan fills out the image by layering it with more and more potent emotional qualities. Next, she enriches and enlarges the image, until it gets so rich and strong that she can almost touch it. When the image becomes "solid" enough — so developed that she can almost touch it and can easily connect with it when she is singing — then she knows she is ready to perform.

Interestingly, as Joan talked about the image becoming richer, her own voice and expression became richer too. She leaned a little more forward as she described the image becoming larger. Her skin softened and her eyes brightened as she described the image becoming rich enough. Her whole expression transformed and I felt myself drawn in; I began to see an image, too, stunning, fascinating, and beautiful.

I realized that though Joan's skill was intuitive, it was developed with methodical, common-sense logic. Before the performance, she deliberately built the images and feelings that would affect her music appropriately. Then she placed them into the performance situation so that she could re-experience them as she performed. I had an impression of her walking onto the stage, slipping into a special concentration where her images, like stained glass windows, colored her music with their nuance. I felt this was the source of her impact.

By contrast, I thought of other performers I've known, who absently drag into their performances haunting images of the audience rejecting them, or of their teachers scolding them, or images and feelings of intense fear, competitiveness, frustration. I was positive these negative images were harming their music–making.

Over the last few years, many teachers — Joan Wall, Joan Dornemann, Janet Bookspan, Wesley Balk, Eloise Ristad, and Barry Green, to name a few — have begun producing results in the previously nebulous area of performing. Though they all have their unique approach, they all pursue refining the inner experience of the performer rather than simply prescribing a correct, authoritative description of how the music should sound. Their ideas have brought the matter of what a performer thinks and feels during her performance closer to a level of skill rather than chance.

Some of their ideas resemble acting methods and character-building schemes: imagining purposes, motivations, and emotions to intertwine with the music. Others direct their students to do anything that would shake a little life into the stifled inner atmosphere of a musician while performing: cluck like a chicken, slither like a snake, bounce like a pogo stick. Even these hit-or-miss techniques produce results because the more lively the inner experiences of the performer, the more lively the resulting performances.

Under their direction, performers begin to shine on stage, achieving significant improvements in their performances.The performer's new inner experiences often produce dramatic and enabling changes not only in his or her "stage presence," but in the performer's instrumental or vocal technique as well. Difficult passages suddenly ripple out with ease; strenuous high notes suddenly seem lower and easier to handle; nuances in phrasing naturally develop — all without ever mentioning technique or interpretation.

Over the last twelve years I've devoted my work to developing a comprehensive approach to many of these performance techniques so that musicians can handle this dimension of their work as easily as possible. In addition to the teachers mentioned above, the work of Dr. Herbert Benson, Dr. Milton Erickson, Dr. Genie LaBourde, Dr. John Grinder, and Dr. Richard Bandler have all had a strong impact on my approach. I have also borrowed heavily from the work of pioneers in sports psychology, especially their techniques developed for training Olympic athletes. Many of the techniques for attaining optimum performance in athletics adapt quite well to musical performance. My purpose was to uncover the essentials of these different techniques and to make them easy to use and applicable to each musician's individuality.

Performance work — the time spent to craft a rich inner experience to take into the performance — is essential because a correct interpretation played with correct technique is simply not enough to build a powerful performance; like Joan Wall creating rich, refined, emotional images to heighten her performances, the performer must build compelling inner experiences beforehand and take them into the performance. This inner work is practical and necessary for any performer, and is ultimately the source of the performer's artistry. Technical work, interpretive work, and this kind of performance work are each vital to the performance. They all affect the final performance the audience experiences.

I'd like to introduce some of the performers you will meet in this book. All of them are talented musicians who transformed their performances through the various techniques presented in this book. They were all facing unique performance situations, just as you will; reading of their success, you will get an idea of how to apply the techniques to your own situations.

## Sally

Sally was a college student in voice. Though not a nervous performer, she generally gave bland performances. She hated being passed over at auditions and special events, especially when she had worked hard and accomplished what she had set out to do.

## Shirley

Shirley loved music but experienced her performances as unpleasant struggles with herself. In the practice room, she could play beautifully, but the idea of playing with so much expression in front of an audience hurled her into demanding expectations, gripping confusion, and dried up musical feelings. She secretly wished she could simply enjoy performing.

## Richard

Richard had just arranged his new performance schedule. For the first time in his career, he would be able to support himself giving classical concerts. However, with more music to learn than he ever had before, he found himself missing his rehearsals, playing rigidly, and experiencing other threatening interferences.

## Marilyn

Marilyn, an organist, was hired to perform for a ceremony honoring a newly installed organ at a university. Many important people would be there. It was an opportunity she had dreamed of. However, she found she could not get herself together and dreaded the performance.

## Pat

Pat became terrified when she had to perform in auditions and in front of an audience. She desperately wanted to perform because she loved to sing, but she fell apart, especially in front of important people. She felt she had more on the inside, but didn't know how to get it.

## Jim

Jim's musical sensitivity was extremely developed. He loved music, but experienced frustration in his work. He eventually stopped playing due to the intense unpleasantness.

All of these musicians, for one reason or another, felt they would not be able to conjure the energy, the charisma, and the command of the stage necessary for their performances. They felt — rightly — that their stage fright, or nerves, or lack of confidence would result in a dismal experience for themselves and the audience.

When I helped them apply the techniques described in this book to their performance approach, these performers took command of the stage and their music. They learned to commit one hundred percent of themselves to their performances. And since our work together, they have expanded the principles of the techniques and adapted them for their individual needs, and have continued to work as successful performers, busily managing their artistry on stage, and thereby enriching their own and the audience's lives. Now this book will help you do what I helped them do.

# I

# THE ART OF PERFORMING MUSIC

When we study music, we study the objective parts of music — ear training, theory, sightreading, technique, and interpretation. But where do we learn to make something special happen in a performance, to involve ourselves in the music, to ignite our performances with fire, depth, or sensitivity? Creating inspired performances is the most important subject for us musicians who want to share our music, yet who can tell us much about how to do it? Perhaps part of the problem is that the subjective qualities of performing — charisma, presence, nerves, stage fright, tension, conviction — have been considered separately as psychological events or as matters of personality and treated as though they have nothing to do with studying music. Yet, these qualities profoundly influence the way we make our music. In fact, I find they are the wellspring of our artistry.

At one of my performance workshops, Gretchen, with a hopeless look on her face, told me that she wanted to share her music and to sing well. When I asked her

## Examine All Forms of Performing

what prevented her from achieving this, she said, "My breath is not working right. I'm not supporting the tone right. I think the tension in the back of my neck is holding back the tone."

Her complaints were not uncommon to hear among singers and other musicians. I elaborated, "You hear that your voice doesn't sound right. You know that you need to fix the breath, fix the tone, fix the tension —"

She was nodding her head emphatically. These were definitely the thoughts that distracted her when she sang.

"— but let's look at a larger idea of performing," I resumed. "Let's get an example of top performance — let's consider rock musicians. I can think of a successful rock group who smashes their guitars as part of their act," I suggested. I knew that bringing up rock musicians as an example for top performing would surprise Gretchen, but I've found that different kinds of performing share a common thread, and I encourage performers to look beyond their own area of study. It can make it easier to distinguish what is important about performing.

Gretchen tilted her head and looked at me through the corners of her eyes, skeptical about what I was saying. Her expression implied, "What does smashing guitars have to do with singing opera?"

I continued, "Imagine for a moment what might be lost if when they are smashing their guitars against their Peavy amps they worry to themselves 'Oh, I hope I am swinging my guitar right' or 'I wonder if I am supporting the swing with the proper stance?'"

She grinned a bit and pulled her chin in, a sign she was considering my argument.

"Isn't an opera singer who quizzes herself about whether or not she is using her voice correctly *as she sings* losing as much as a rock musician who quizzes himself about how he swings his guitar as he smashes it?" I asked. "Either way, a quality of one hundred percent committment would be lost."

She conceded my point but wondered, "How do you get the voice, the breath, the resonance all working together?"

"Consider this: when they are all working together, is part of you worrying about your breath, your diction, or your tone?" I asked.

"No...no," she said softly. I could see her considering my question.

"*Something* is different when it is all working together, something *other* than constantly worrying about your technique. When you are not worrying about your technique, you are *doing something else*," I suggested.

Gretchen took a deep breath. I could see by her crinkled forehead that she was thinking about it, concentrating.

"Even a beginning student can captivate an audience — not because of her technical skill, but because of ...?" I prodded.

She rearranged herself in her chair, leaned back and clasped her hands together, and then shifted her posture again. I could almost see by this motion that an insight was working its way through Gretchen's mind. "I know what you mean," she said at last. "I've seen children perform simple pieces of music, and they were graceful and beautiful — even when they were just beginning." She paused a moment. "I think it's the way the child feels about the performance and the music, about herself ... about a lot of things."

I saw her eyes defocus and the corner of her lips lift into a gentle smile. Her fluid expression suggested that she knew she was right on track. Her agitated ideas about her technique were slowing down and quieting in her mind. She had just expressed the realization that, in addition to technical achievment, how a person feels about her music, about herself, about everything on stage are also important for performance excellence.

I wanted to help her consider that realization. "Not only with a child, but with *every* musician," I stressed. "It's the experience on the inside of a musician while she is performing that makes a difference." She had seen in my master classes that when the musicians get their inner experience in order, and clear away their distractions, then they can make a human to human connection with the audience and the beauty of the music can come flowing through. "Without having their inner experience in order, their performance suffers, regardless of how advanced their vocal technique is. It is as though performance skills are the skills of preparing yourself — your whole inner experience — for the time you are performing so that you *can* commit one hundred percent to the performance." Gretchen was ready to explore this in greater depth.

## Performance Skills

In these and other master classes, the musicians and I pursue the basic idea that performing skills are quite different from technical skills, or even interpretation skills. We find repeatedly that the performers' inner experiences directly affect their technical execution and their interpretation. We break away from the idea that perfected technical execution will always lead to brilliant performing. We also conclude that arranging an individualistic interpretation — tempo selection, placement of crescendos and decrescendos, and so on — will not always add up to a stirring performance. In our classes, we establish the following three characteristics shared by excellent performers and use them as our guidelines to build a performance, to use them in *addition* to technical and interpretive work.

## Resolve Your Inner Conflicts for 100% Commitment

Top performers are conflict-free at the time of their performance; every shred of their energy is committed to what they are doing. And, because no internal interruptions sap the energy needed for what they are doing on stage, their naturalness and involvement surpass those of other performers.

Stage fright is an example of a major conflict, but a conflict can also be as subtle as the slight feeling of forgetting something while walking out of the door and not knowing what it is. It can be a concern about having a memory slip, or of not having enough time to prepare, or of not hitting a high note. Performers with inner conflicts while on stage are the ones who fail. As one side of their conflict pulls for one thing and the other side of their conflict pulls for another, the energy to commit to their performance is divided. Regardless of their vocal or instrumental technique level, their performances don't succeed because they are not organized on the inside to completely commit to what they are doing.

Top performers desire their performances; their bodies, minds, and music all fuse together in an atmosphere of volition. Something about the performance beckons with desirability and compels them to perform. They love the music, the finesse of pulling off a tricky passage, the beauty, the crowd, the fame, or the risk — it could be any aspect of the performance that they love, but it tantalizes them and they are always plugged into it.

It is surprising how many performers have not thought about how their distaste for an aspect of a performance situation will negatively affect their performances. Obviously, performers who dislike something about a certain performance situation will have a hard time mustering the command of what is happening on stage. They may not like the music, the style of preparation, the pay, the conductor, the intensity — it could be anything — but as long as the performers expect an unpleasant experience, the desire to perform will be absent. Their performances won't be very compelling to them, and they will not commit one hundred percent.

Top performers during their performance experience an inner condition that is rich and fascinating, and that results in a "larger than life" or "commanding" quality. A great deal of activity is happening on the inside — all varied, complex, and highly energized. If you were

### Discover What Compels You

*Top performers desires their performances; ...*

### Infuse Your Performing with Intensity

to drop inside a top performer during the peak of his or her performance, you would be stunned by the intensity and richness of what he or she feels.

I find that these three characteristics can describe all top musical performers, whether they play or sing classical, pop, jazz, or any other kind of music, and whether they are beginners or highly skilled professionals.

These qualities can put a handle on the otherwise elusive character of brilliance in performance and they lead to practical guidelines for improving performance:

1) If your performing is riddled with conflicts, you will need to resolve the conflicts.

2) If your performing lacks qualities you can commit to, then you will need to develop qualities worth committing to.

3) If your performing is colorless and limp, then you will need to enrich or enlarge it.

**What to Work On**

Using the techniques described in this book, we will pursue these characteristics. In my classes we seek out and resolve conflicts, determine what genuinely attracts the performer and weave it into the music-making, and refine and enrich those desires. In other words, we "tune up" the performer's internal experience until it is conflict free, compelling, and rich — and the results are astounding.

You can tune your inner experiences too. This kind of work will lead outside of traditional music preparation.

Your conflicts that need resolution can originate far beyond the typical concerns about your music. What you value and find worth committing to — worth desiring — can also extend beyond the boundaries of the music and will certainly be unique to you. And how you build intensity can also be surprisingly far from a traditional musical exercise.

Tuning yourself toward performing without conflicts, toward what you desire, and toward what is rich will also lead you to a unique performance. Top performers exude their individuality during their performances precisely because their performances reflect their unique experiences. Tina Turner no doubt enjoys a completely different inner experience while performing pop music than Marilyn Horne experiences while performing opera, but they both deliver powerful performances because they each tune themselves until everything about the performance fits them like a glove.

Let's consider how a performer who tunes his internal condition so that it is conflict-free, compelling, and rich will achieve a good performance. In the absence of any internal conflicts, all of a performer's expressions will appear to work together — even the subtleties of her skin tone, breathing rate, and movements. These subtle changes in her overall appearance will correspond to subtle changes in her sound.

The audience will see and hear the synchronization of these nuances, and, as they empathize with the performer, they will begin to sense their own inner experience synchronizing, too. They will feel the performer's undiluted concentration and they will begin to concentrate as well. This quality of concentration on the part of the performer can transform a crowd into a single empathizing entity so involved you can hear the proverbial pin drop, or so involved that the applause after the last note is delayed while the audience, stunned, struggles to regain their sense of self. These are the memorable performances.

The Audience Echoes Your Level of Concentration

ROBERT CALDWELL

*The performer's job description could read 'build a congruent, compelling, and potent internal state and take it into the performance.'*

If, on the other hand, a performer is full of conflicts, this too will show through his expressions — both visibly and audibly. His conflicting urges will create subtle shifts in his movements, breathing, and sounds and they will appear out of sync. The audience will sense the incongruence, too, even if it is very slight. They will not be able to identify with the performer and, because the performer is sending out mixed signals, they will not be led to a high-quality experience. Under these conditions, even when the music is technically perfect, the audience will not get what they came for.

In this way, the undiluted, cohesive, rich internal state of the performer is the main event of the performance. It is the beginning movement, like a flick on a row of dominoes, that initiates the performance, infuses the performer, the music, the atmosphere on stage, the hall, and finally the inner states of the audience with its qualities. Any pure, desired, rich state from within a musician's experience can work — states of happiness, excitement, fascination, beauty, humor, compassion, complexity — which is why there is such a wide variety of successful performers and styles of music. Whether any of these states succeed in the performance, though, depends in part upon whether they are conflict-free. The internal experience must also be compelling and rich.

The task of preparing your inner experience this way for your performances presents quite a challenge, which is perhaps why there are so few top performers. Your perception of the world, your personality, your orientation to what makes music beautiful or meaningful are all complex. Sometimes tuning your inner experience requires a delicate vagueness — a subtle sensibility — because the deliberateness can interfere with it, just as deliberately trying to get to sleep can interfere with falling asleep. Or perhaps a conflict is so familiar it is hard to recognize.

Yet even in this suggestive, elusive, and challenging work, you can manage the intangible qualities of your personality and can put them together to build an appropriate state, one that will enable you to connect with the music, commit one hundred percent, and make something special happen in your music.

It seemed that only a couple of short weeks had passed after my talk with Gretchen. She and I had worked with many of the techniques and ideas described in this book. She had prepared her inner experience for her time on stage. She had learned how to resolve her conflicts about her voice and performing and how to emphasize what was important to her about her music and her performing as she sang. Rather than harping on whether her technique was working correctly or not, she learned to fill her experience with what was special to her, and it helped her to actually reach her technical goals.

When Gretchen's final turn came up to sing, she had a twinkle in her eyes. She walked to the piano with a distinct lilt, a poise. I was already feeling pleased for her. Even at this point, it was obvious she was going to give a great performance. As she began to sing, a glow spread through her body and a warm silky tone colored her voice and sounded with three times the volume and just as much ease. Her inner involvement captivated us. We became enchanted as the moment-by-moment charge of the music swirled around us. The instant she finished, the class spontaneously cheered. She had given the performance her all, and it was beautiful. It was magic.

# II

# Imagining the Performance

Your performance begins in your imagination. If you look toward your future performance and see something dreadful, your image of the performance will not be one you can commit to one hundred percent — who would commit to something dreadful? If you see a vague idea of your performance, it will not inspire you. However, if you see a rich performance, full of what you want, it certainly will influence your work favorably. And if you see an intense, vast image of the performance that covers everything about the performance, and is so embued with qualities you deeply desire that you are physically drawn to it, you will very likely achieve those qualities and will deliver a beautiful performance.

LEONARDO da VINCI

*It is of no small benefit on finding oneself in bed in the dark to go over again in the imagination the main outlines of the forms previously studied, or of other noteworthy things conceived by ingenious speculation.*

So, as musicians, our first work is to imagine our performance in such a way that draws us towards it. We need an entire concept of the performance. A performer may only imagine one part of the performance with intensity — his technique or memorization, for example — and ignore the rest. Though his technique may shine, his performance will nevertheless remain lifeless simply because the other parts of his performance are absent or sagging in his imagination. He needs to expand his attention beyond just his technique and breathe his imagination into the entire performance experience. He needs to imagine how he will be involved in the music, how his performance will be meaningful, or how he will feel after the performance, for example. He needs to imagine the full scope of the performance. Just by including everything, he can eliminate many of the struggles and tensions that would otherwise occur in the performance.

You will probably find it quite challenging to imagine a performance completely, to prepare every aspect, to render every concern. Maybe you don't know what kind of performer you want to be. Maybe you don't know what music to select or how to respond to the person in charge of the concert or audition. Maybe you can only imagine the performance as a blurry, muffled smear on a dark stage. But then, this is your performance work — to shine a bright, clear light on every aspect of the performance, to address every one of your concerns, and to tailor each one into something you genuinely desire so that, in the end, everything about the performance fits you like a glove. Then, complete commitment will naturally follow, the music will hit its peak, and you will deliver a powerful performance.

In this chapter, I will introduce the Action/Outcome Grid, a tool to help you imagine everything about your performance. It will help direct you to the many parts of your performance that you should give your attention to and develop the outcomes for your performance that will inspire you. The grid is a combination of the Issues in Performance and the Four Stages of Performance.

## Issues in Performance

The first step is to map out *all* of your performance issues. How to handle a certain phrase, develop your technique, manage your concentration are examples of issues of your performance. Look at the list of issues described below and over the next few pages. Notice that they fall into a pattern, more or less, of broad issues that progressively become narrow, specific ones. The sample questions and answers are some of the ways that you can stimulate your imagination to find what genuinely attracts you.

What kind of Musician do you want to be?

    Musician

A kind of sage; a refined technician; a scholarly type who would fit into a university setting; a probing genius; a maverick; a celebrity?

What kind of Performer do you want to be?

    Performer

A fiery type; passionate, relentless; a world traveler; a generous friend; an authoritative, commanding leader; a spellbinder; emotional; a well–prepared, proficient performer; an inspired performer?

What do you want in performing?

    Performing
    in General

Easy, comfortable performing; style, grace and charm; a sense of importance, urgency, drive; altruism, dedication; matter–of–fact resolve, professionalism?

## This Particular Performance

What do you want to happen for this particular performance?

> Win the prize; set the stage with balance or flash or majesty; project to the balcony; get through the jury; get the role, job, or record contract; reach a personal artistic peak?

## Parts of the Performance

*Think of the Parts of the Performance as issues about your compositions, your dress, the time and place of your performance, your invitations, your reception, your time on stage before, between, and after the music. By isolating the order and substance of everything the audience will see and hear during your performance, you will generate a full list of the parts of your performance. The column on the right is a sample list. These are all matters you will have to contend with. Your unique performance may include several not listed here. Work them out so that they suit you personally.*

What do you want at each individual part of the performance?

*Warming up*

How do you want to warm up before the performance?

> Slowly; emotionally, as well as physically; with a pre-set routine; for a few minutes, and then a pause; in a reverie?

*Walking out on stage*

How do you want to walk out on stage?

> With energy, with charm, with focus, with exuberance?

*Greeting the audience*

How do you want to greet the audience?

> With directness, friendliness, an elaborate bow, earnestness?

*Preparing to play*

How do you want to prepare to play or sing?

With a pause to get your self
together, to jump right into the
music, with a sense of excitement?

*Playing the compositions*

What compositions do you want to perform?

Deep probing pieces, pieces you
love, feel challenged by, fit your
personality?

What order do you want to perform them in?

Arrange the pieces so they provide a
sense of harmonic, emotional, or
dramatic  balance, lightness, or
depth?

What special outcomes do you have for each piece?

Perform the first piece with a lot of
love or compassion;  close the last
piece with every ounce of energy
you have?

*Leaving the stage*

How do you want to leave the stage?

With a sense of triumph,
satisfaction, poise, friendliness,
forthrightness?

*Recovering at the intermission*

How do you want to use the time at intermission?

To relax, to greet people backstage,
to distract yourself, to organize
yourself, to review your
performance?

Also consider questions about the audience, how they are invited, who you want present; about your performance dress and the messages you want to convey; about the reception and the atmosphere, food served, and duration. Any of these could become a source of interference with your commitment if not worked out to your satisfaction.

## Parts
## of the Parts

*Work your imagination on even the smaller, more detailed parts of the performance. For example, under the subject of your compositions, work out what you want in each opening, each passage, each phrase, or develop your ideas about the interpretation of each piece. Under the subject of your audience, work out the promotion, the invitations, the program notes. Under greeting the audience, work out your introduction to your pieces, should you have one. Under the clothes you will wear, work out where you will shop, how much you will spend.*

What do you want to happen in the parts of the parts? How do you want to handle them?

Master the difficult passage in measure 40 in the third piece; articulate the harmonic movement in measure 20 in the first piece; profoundly render the ending of the piece just before intermission?

*Note*
Because *technique* and *interpretation* are applicable to specific phrases as well as general levels of achievement, you can think of them as parts of the parts, as general qualities of a Musician, or as issues of their own.

Musician

Performer

Performing

This
Performance

Parts of the
Performance

Parts
of the Parts

This list could become more and more specific. Certainly other issues that concern you about your performance defy words and would be difficult to classify. But notice that almost any issue about your performance can fit into a scale that measures very broad to very specific. It is important to orient yourself to the complete range of issues when preparing for your performance because, like vertebrae along the spine, each issue is necessary to support your performance. None should be left as vague lifeless spots in your imagination. The large ideas of the kind of musician you want to be should be as developed as the specific kind of tone you want to render in the 4th phrase of the second piece.

## Stages of Performance

The performance begins long before you walk out on stage. Special concerns begin the moment you decide to perform and others germinate while you select the music, rehearse the music, perform the music, and then live with the performance afterward. You will have concerns at each stage and each will need to be imagined fully.

| Planning | Rehearsing | Performing | Afterwards |

The Four Stages of Performance

*Planning the Performance and Music*

As you plan the music, your choices should be based on qualities you can commit to, otherwise you may find yourself stuck. If you choose music without enough challenge, you may lose interest, for example, or if you choose music too difficult for you, you may set yourself up for disappointment. You will need to identify and amplify the qualities you want for the music and the rest of the performance as you plan it.

How do you want to plan your performance? What do you want to sketch in your imagination? What will be special about it? What will be attractive to you? What qualities will engage you?

Win an audition; reach an artistic peak; plan music that fits well together; plan a beautiful and comfortable time and place for your audience; excitement; enthusiasm; determination; challenge; richness; realistic rehearsal strategies; video taping?

*Rehearsing for the Performance*

If your rehearsals seem undesirable to you, it probably means that you have other ways to rehearse that you are not using and should. Or it could mean that you have concerns about the first stage of the performance, planning the music and performance, that have not yet been met, such as concerns about choosing music too difficult to learn in the amount of time you have to learn it. These concerns should be worked out so that everything about your rehearsals will be attractive and make sense to you.

How do you want to rehearse the music? How do you want to feel about your rehearsals? What will make them special? How will they support your outcomes? What is your ultimate style?

To set up an hourly schedule; to head for moments of inspiration; to strive to optimize your state of focus and efficiency?

Many performers experience performing as a caldron where they forge their artistic visions. The audience produces a charge that melds their minds, bodies, and sensitivities. They acquire a taste for this condition and learn to savor it. When they learn to create this sensation in their rehearsals, these musicians become very effective performers.

### Performing

What qualities do you want to experience during performing? What qualities would attract you? What about them would electrify you?

Freedom in your body; rich warm colors flooding your imagination; complete involvement in the moment by moment expression of the music; touching the audience with depth of emotion; profound feeling of power?

If you find it difficult to imagine what you want during performing, it probably means that you have another issue that has not been taken care of in the other stages of performing. Perhaps there was not a compelling reason to perform in the first place. Maybe the music required more rehearsal time than was available and this concern was not addressed immediately. Or perhaps the rehearsal period may have been too short or inappropriately directed by someone else. Typically, when you completely work out all the issues of the other stages of performing, the actual performing— what you want to see, how you want to sound, how you want to feel when you walk out on stage — becomes easy to imagine.

*After the Performance*

Some musicians put off performing because they dread the void that comes after the performance. The performance itself seems to them like a dead end, a choke-off point. All of their constant work suddenly ends. Some call the experience "post-performance depression." Sometimes, even, performers feel cheated, as though the performance should have been more meaningful, more rewarding, especially compared to the amount of work required to produce it. Such a condition can be devastating.

How do you want to feel after your performance? What do you want to have accomplished? What would you miss if you didn't perform at all?

"I want my performance to be a step in becoming a proficient and elegant performer;" "I want to look back and feel that my performance was a solid base for future confidence;" "I want to look back and know that I have done my best."

If you imagine what you would like to have after the performance and deliberately place your imaginings where a void could form, it will give you a net, an understanding to ease the transition to your next performance. You can easily bypass feeling depressed or empty.

More importantly, though, imagining what you want after the performance will color the preceeding stages. The process will shape what is meaningful about your performance. One concert pianist, Santiago Rodriguez, plans an interesting transition for his after

JOSE CARRERAS

*... after (the high notes), then yes, the pleasure, the satisfaction of having risen to the challenge, is quite unimaginable...*

performance time. He knows that after a concert his wife will ritually ask him, "Did you leave *everything* on the stage?"and he will work so that he can answer with an enthusiastic, proud "*Yes!*" By wanting and expecting to say *yes* with a particularly inspiring tone, he can plan his performance, rehearse for it, and actually perform it in such a way that he will get it. Imagining a full and rich experience for the time after your performance will help prevent you from wasting time. By knowing what you want after your performance, you can determine what is relevant from what is not and can better plan your efforts.

In my experience, helping performers develop this stage of their performance has had a greater impact than nearly anything else in creating powerful performances. I have also found that this stage is typically the least-imagined among musicians who struggle with their performances. Their imagination of their experience after the performance is like a blank spot with nothing and no one in it. After they fill it with something desirable — anything at all — they become inspired and their performance intensifies.

For the stage *after the performance*, consider different time periods — immediately afterward, the next week, the next month, year, or five years, even ten or twenty years. Ask yourself what you want to have transpired in your performance that would satisfy even your deepest desires. How will you want to look back on the performance from each of these time periods? What will you want your performance filled with that would be the ultimate for you?

## Introducing the Action/Outcome Grid

Examine the Action/Outcome Grid on the next page. You can see that the chart combines each *Issue Level* with each *Stage of the Performance*, which creates a thorough map of the performance. Use it to get a complete idea of what you want to happen — what your desired *outcome* would be — for all phases of the performance. Then use it to help you plan what you need to do to achieve your desired outcomes. The grid will prevent you from ignoring elements of the performance that you should attend to. For example, it will prevent you from focusing *only* on technique and consequently performing like someone who has only focused on technique.

| Action Outcome Grid | Planning | Rehearsing | Performing | Afterward |
|---|---|---|---|---|
| Musician | | | | |
| Performer | | | | |
| Performing | | | | |
| This Performance | | | | |
| Parts of the Performance | | | | |
| Parts of the Parts | | | | |

Sally is a dedicated and conscientious student in graduate school and receives A's in all of her work. In keeping with her diligence, she expertly sets up schedules to prepare herself for her graduate recitals. She proudly displays her elaborate practice schedules, and proudly meets them. Her schedules demand fifteen minutes on the first piece on Monday morning, thirty-five minutes on the second piece on Monday afternoon, or first thirty measures of the third piece on Friday, and so on — all very organized. In her eyes, managing herself to practice regularly means preparing as a musician. She has defined success as sticking to her well-thought-out schedules.

She hits her mark repeatedly and keeps her schedules, a genuine triumph given the general chaos of her life. However, she doesn't understand why she fails to get major parts in the opera productions and why the solo positions in the choir concerts pass her by. Though her music is accurately learned, her performances are devoid of any sublime ideas and emotions, beautiful lines, or general warmth.

If we juxtapose the Action/Outcome Grid over Sally's imagination of her performances, we can easily place her efforts. We see richly developed ideas on the intersection of Parts of the Performance (memorizing the music) and The Rehearsal Stage (her elaborate schedules). About this subject, she knows what she wants, how she will allocate her time, how she will discipline herself, how she will manage herself when her scheduled demands arrive — all very well developed in her imagination. She has even devised alternative strategies to rehearse memorizing her music, in case one doesn't work. She has options, ideas, feelings, attitudes, experience blooming at this intersection.

*Sally rehearsed memorizing the music extremely well. Her outcome Grid might look like the one above. The other intersections would not be developed.*

However, the rest of her Action/Outcome Grid has blank spots all over it. If she were asked what she wants out of performing music in the first place, she would not know what to say. She would draw a blank. If she were asked what her ultimate desire is for after the performance, her ideas would be dim. If asked about any of the other points on the Grid, she would find colorless or blank notions. Her mark, her concept of a successful performance, simply does not include enough of the performance.

Jim, in contrast to Sally, can articulate musical ideas that are highly developed. His passion for the sublime experiences of beauty is deeply felt. His ear for discriminating what is beautiful from what is not is delicately calibrated. His understanding of how music can convey the depths of human emotion is fully embraced. When he goes to play the piano, however, his technique is ill-equipped to handle his big, rich musical ideas. His performances are reduced to moments of beauty that slip through the clumsy handling of the keys.

Superimposing the Action/Outcome Grid over Jim's imagination of his performances, we see the top rows of the grid fully in bloom in his imagination. The large ideas of why music is important and sublime, of how it is meaningful to communicate beauty are vibrant in his mind. But the lower rows, the more narrowly focused issues, like *This Performance*, or *Parts of the Parts* (technique) appear as dim, vague spots. His imagination of the physical sensations of executing his profound, beautiful ideas with his hands are dull. In contrast to Sally, his ideas about rehearsing appear as a series of lifeless images. Other smaller parts of the parts, such as the style of walking on and off stage, of bowing, of greeting the audience, of talking to the audience afterward are perhaps completely absent.

Both Sally and Jim's performances need to expand beyond the issues they have focused on. Their performances suffer simply because they work their imaginations on only a few issues and omit or vaguely imagine the others.

The Action/Outcome Grid is a planning tool to ensure that you consider each issue, from broad to specific, at each stage of your performance. It creates a map of the overall dimensions of your performance — the sublime, as well as the practical requirements — and, like a blueprint, it provides an overview of your entire performance and your preparation for it.

## Using the Action/Outcome Grid

The Action/Outcome Grid is like a map for a traveler showing the destination and the routes that lead there: it is used to refer to when building your performance, to orient you to all the aspects of your performance, to guide you toward your destination.

### An Evaluation Tool

Look at each intersection and evaluate the condition of your imagination about that subject, your outcome as you perceive it. At some intersections, you may find that you do not have a clue about what you want. At others, you may find rich ideas, but riddled with conflicts. Or you may find rich and compelling ideas, feelings, experiences, full of what you want, and no conflicts. Knowing the condition of your imaginings will enable you to direct your work: to search for what genuinely compels you; to resolve any conflicts; and to intensify the qualities you desire. Remember, the ultimate goal is to reach a state where you know what you want, have no conflicts about it, and are compelled to accomplish it.

RICHARD MILLER

*...no matter what the technical orientation or level of skill, a pessimistic singer is not a successful singer; mental attitude can make or break a career. The singer who has acquired free physical responses, who has digested the poem, the dramatic situation, and the musical idiom, and who feels compelled to express personal reactions through the amalgamation of body, word, and imagination, should enter confidently into the act of performance, believing in its rightness.*

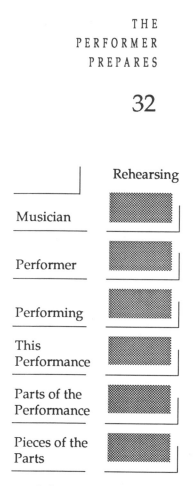

Rehearsing

Musician

Performer

Performing

This
Performance

Parts of the
Performance

Pieces of the
Parts

Sally could have expanded her ideas of how to rehearse memorizing the music by climbing up the issue levels on the grid and asking herself how she wanted to rehearse for this performance, for performing in general, as a performer, and, finally, as a musician in general. She would have tapped into how she would rehearse the larger, sublime ideas of music, as well as the practical ideas of rehearsing. Each of these intersections could have been as richly formulated as her elaborate rehearsal schedules.

Let's use Sally for an example of how she could have used the grid to evaluate her performance. She already works her imagination about rehearsing and fills her mind profusely with ideas, concepts, and patterns of work that will effectively get her music learned. If she looks at the intersection of *Parts of the Performance* and *Rehearsing*, she would see that she has indeed developed this intersection, especially the part *learning the music*.

Next, she can step up the column of Rehearsing to the next issue level and ask herself how she wants to rehearse for *This Performance*. She probably finds some overlap of ideas about how she will rehearse the sections of her music. But the larger ideas of *This Performance* will not be developed. Instead of just *learning the music*, this particular performance could also become a test for herself, an opportunity to reach a personal milestone in expressiveness, or an experiment to find out whether she can keep the thread of her attention from beginning to end of her performance. These broader ideas, when tailored to her personality and coupled with her developed ideas about memorizing the sections of music, would begin to substantially expand her imagining of her performance.

Next she can move up another issue level to the intersection of *Performer* and *Rehearsing*, and ask herself how she wants to rehearse as a performer in general. She would find that her ideas at this point are substantially weaker than rehearsing her memorizing. Compared to her teeming, rich, detailed, and compelling images of her rehearsal schedules, her image of herself as a performer in general would appear fuzzy, dim, colorless. She may have a few ideas about rehearsing as a *diligent student*, but not as a *compelling performer*.

Pursuing the subject of rehearsing as a performer, she might begin to wander into some abstract ideas. Maybe she could imagine herself as a fiery performer and then decide this doesn't suit her. Maybe the kind of performer who *warms the stage* really hits her desire. And then she can ask herself how she would rehearse in order to successfully *warm the stage,* and begin to fill her imagination with ideas.

Next she can step up to *Musician* and *Rehearsing*. Here her ideas of the kind of musician she wants to be and how that kind of musician would rehearse would be nearly absent in her imagination. She would need to fill these gaps. She could develop multifaceted ideas of herself as a musician rehearsing with as much intensity as her ideas of her elaborate schedules and see images of herself being demanding, or becoming involved in the music, or expressing deep professionalism or probing creativity — or perhaps see herself in all these ways. And, if she is attracted to any or all of these outcomes, she can ask herself how she would rehearse as that kind of musician.

By using the Action/Outcome Grid to address each one of the intersections, Sally can evaluate the condition of her imagination about her performance and can find her weak spots. Using the techniques described later in this book, she can then develop her imagination wherever it is weak. This work will ultimately add depth and nuance to her flat performances.

*A Tool to Prompt Your Imagination*

Look over the Action/Outcome Grid and you may recognize for yourself some areas that are richly developed and other areas that are blank or weak. If you come to an intersection that seems blank , you will need to put something desirable there. Fill out your imagination. The questions below will prompt your imagination of your ideal experience for that intersection.

For example, at the intersection of *Musician* and *Performing*, you could ask yourself, "As a *Musician*, what do I want during *Performing*? Confidence? Ease? Passion?" Then imagine yourself with confidence and then with ease, and finally with passion and decide which one is more appealing.

Or you can ask yourself "What kind of Musician do I want to be during Performing? Do I want to perform

For some people, it may help to take a blank sheet of paper and actually draw a grid. At each intersection, ask yourself what you want for that intersection and write down your ideas. Some people use index cards, one for each intersection, and write their outcomes on them. Or others stick post-em notes on a large poster board.

like a well–trained professional? Like a sensitive artist? Like a probing, deep philosopher? Or like a fiery, charismatic rebel?" Again, explore these qualities in your imagination.

Or you can ask "What would happen if I performed like a confident musician? Or passionate? Or sensitive?"

Use these questions and any others you may devise to stimulate your imagination, to speculate on what your choices might be. Each choice will stimulate different ideas. For example, compare confidence and passion. As a *confident* musician, how would you plan the music? How would you rehearse? How would you perform? How would you evaluate yourself after the performance? Notice what might change as a *passionate* musician. Would you select the same music, rehearse the same way, perform the same way, feel the same way after the performance?

*A Tool to Follow-Through on Each Issue*

Use the grid to thoroughly cover every issue through all four stages of the performance. For example, look at *Parts of the Performance*, and consider *walking out onto the stage*. This part of the performance is often overlooked and underdeveloped. The initial appearance on stage casts an impression on the audience that is difficult to change, so it needs to work. Janet Bookspan, a highly effective performance coach and director, will spend considerable time and energy helping a performer learn many approaches to walking out on stage — to the great benefit of the performance — because it sets up both the performer and the audience. As Bookspan says, it is far easier to keep the audience's interest than to regain it once it is lost. This is an artistic concern and no trivial part of the performance.

Using the grid, you can comprehensively cover the issue about *walking out on stage* by considering it through all four Stages of the Performance. Consider how you want to plan *walking out on stage*. What about it will be significant? Do you want to project an aura of confidence? of welcome? of happiness? of aloofness? of excitement?

Next consider how you would rehearse *walking out on stage*. You might want to practice several different trials in front of a teacher, coach, or mock audience. You might want to develop different attitudes to walk out on stage with, so that you increase your range of choices, rather than decide on only one. You may want to feel spontaneous, alert, and friendly. Joan Wall sometimes asks her students to rehearse saying to themselves, just before they walk out, "I'm glad I'm here and I'm glad you are here," as a simple, but effective cue to slip into an appropriate state.

Next, how would you perform *walking out on stage*? How will you handle the shift from greeting the audience to concentrating on performing the music? Some performers take forever staring at the floor, wetting their lips, tuning their instruments; others step right into the performance. What will work for you? What is your ideal? And how will you have rehearsed it?

Finally, consider how you want to feel after the performance about your *walking out on stage*. Feel proud about it? Do you want it to become a cue, a way of triggering pleasantness for future performances? Perhaps you will want to learn to excite the audience merely by your walk onstage, even before you play or sing a note?

These may seem like a lot of questions to ask yourself about *walking out on stage*, but considering them all will prevent you from foolishly handling this part of the performance. It is a significant part of the performance and you will need to develop it to suit your desires; otherwise, your entrance will be an indiscriminate compulsion and not an artistic choice. Apologizing, fidgeting, engaging in major internal discussions while walking out on stage are examples of compulsions which are typically not desirable for either the audience or the performer. Use the grid to

This thorough planning is different from rigidly choreographing your entrance. Knowing what you want to accomplish actually frees you to become spontaneous. The richer your ideas, the more likely they will digest into your presence, your automatic functioning, and operate out of your awareness.

stimulate your choices, to sketch out your options.

Peruse the entire grid to stimulate your imagination. Use the intersections to address each of the issues and your concerns about them. Fabricate the ideas of what you want and breathe them into something desirable. Fantasize, pretend, brainstorm, role play — do anything but do not leave these parts of the performance dim, unimagined, unresolved, and, worst of all, undesired.

### A Tool to Spot Conflicts in Your Overall Imagining of the Performance

Another important purpose of the grid is to spot conflicts in the overall concept of the performance, up and down the columns of the Issue Levels, and across the rows of Stages of the Performance. To illustrate, let me describe a lesson with one of my students, Barbara, who struggled to smooth out the scales in the Mozart piano sonata in B flat, K 570. She was frustrated — everything about the scales bothered her. When I asked her how she wanted to play the scales, she said she wanted to *perform the scales with exuberance, ease, and fluidity.*

Notice that *playing scales* is an issue that fits on the grid under *Parts of the Parts.* It is a technical issue and, along with memorizing, fingering, interpreting, it is a part of the piece of music, which is part of overall performance. We could have worked at the same issue level — *Parts of Parts* (technique)— and focused on hand position, fingering, arm weight or other technical ideas. But as another option, we moved up to a broader issue, to that of *Musician.* What kind of musician did she want to be while playing scales in Mozart?

Responding to this question, Barbara discovered a

basic conflict. Part of her seemed to think the kind of musician that played exuberant scales was not the same kind that played Mozart well. A musician who played Mozart well, it seemed, *should* be dignified, someone who mercilessly labored and exhausted herself while striving for the "perfection" always talked about as necessary for playing Mozart.

Obviously, she harbored a conflict in the qualities she was trying to capture in her playing: exuberance in the scales, and dutiful perfectionism in her attitude as a musician. And, though subtle, the conflict was showing up in her technique.

Once uncloaked, the image of being a striving perfectionistic musician was not at all desirable to Barbara. The image was not one she had deliberately chosen. It had just been sitting there, left over from something she'd absorbed or formulated long ago. What Barbara actually *wanted* was to enjoy the gaiety and exuberance of the runs in Mozart.

She discarded the old stuffy idea and replaced it with the kind of musician she could commit to — a musician who played Mozart with joy and exuberance. Even as we talked, I could sense the change. It was subtle, but her face had flushed slightly. Now, the broad issue — the kind of musician she wanted to be — supported the more narrow issue of how to play the scales. As soon as she began playing the scale passages, they immediately became more pliant, almost elastic, and incredibly even and expressive. It was quite astonishing. The incongruity was no longer an obstacle for her.

You can often find incongruities by sliding your perception of the performance up and down the columns of Issue levels and across the rows of the Four Stages of Performing. For example, if part of you wants to be a stately and dignified *Performer* (broad issue), but another

Ernistine Schumann-

Heink

*In everything I do I
have always followed
my instincts... I never
study the part as some
artists do, before a
mirror... acting it out,
looking this way and
that... No, I never
could then... and I
never can go through
with the rehearsal
properly. They always
say that I am absent-
minded, inattentive.
But that isn't really
so. I am really think-
ing all the time of the
points I want to make,
and working it out in
my own mind. So
very often, when I
seem so dumb at
rehearsal, I surprise
them all at the perfor-
mance!*

part of you wants to impress a conductor in the audience by performing with flair for *This Performance* (narrower issue), then the two parts are going to be in conflict and the audience will pick it up. While part of you would be working for dignity and stateliness, another part of you would be working for flair. Or, as another example, part of you may want to plan challenging music for your performance, but you may not have time to rehearse it.

Other conflicts can arise if you believe that there is a "right" outcome for each point of the grid. Perhaps you think you *should* be a *dignified* performer, although you personally want to think of yourself as an *exuberant* performer, as in the example of Barbara. Or perhaps you think you *should* rehearse every day at a certain hour, but with your unique sensibilities, you may accomplish a lot more by rehearsing at odd hours, for odd lengths of time. Every great performer is unique, precisely because each has come to terms with his or her own individual way to handle these issues. You will make your unique choices at each point, too. Push your imagination towards what suits you. Forget the way it *should* be if it doesn't fit you.

The grid will help you survey the performance territory, the field where your inner concerns germinate with the outer concerns of the performance. Use the grid as a guide to till your imagination, to unearth *all* of your concerns, and to plant the ideas of what you want so that the entire performance blooms with the richest expressions of your artistry.

The next section describes how to draw the appropriate qualities from yourself to enrich your outcomes. It offers concepts and skills that will make it easy to work your imagination, to help you find what you want, and bring it all together at the time and place of the performance.

# III

# REFINING
# THE
# PERFORMANCE

Going through the grid and imagining what you want at each point of the performance is probably the most important step in building a successful performance. It will help develop a full-blown image of the entire performance.

Once you have perused the Action/Outcome Grid, the next steps are to 1) refine your outcomes and 2) turn them into actual experiences to take into the performance. These are the steps where you begin to tune your inner state.

To illustrate the idea of tuning yourself, look at figure 2 on the next page, which describes several categories of the inner state of the performer. Each of these categories will offer different pieces of your overall inner state.

| Category | Description |
|---|---|
| Outcome | The representation of what you want to happen. Represents the qualities, the desired experience, the style of what you want. In essence, your artistry. Can be richly developed or poorly developed. |
| Beliefs:<br>   1) about possibility<br>   2) about meaningfulness to you,<br>      your support group<br>      and your audience<br>   3) about identity | 1) *possibility* — a belief that the outcome is not just a pie-in-the-sky desire.<br>2) *meaningfulness* — a belief that the outcome is relevant.<br>3) *identity*—a belief of what and how you could and would perform. |
| Values | A sense of readiness to commit because the performance is perceived as valuable. A strong sense of what is important and what is not. Intense levels of committment in performing require the outcome be perceived as valuable. |
| Emotions | An overall feeling about what you are doing. Normally unconscious. In performing, calmness has often been stressed, regardless of the desired outcome. A wide range of other emotions may fit the outcome better. |
| State of Mind | The flow of thoughts. Internal dialogue, daydreaming, concentration, focus are all examples of states of mind. |
| Physiology | The feeling in the body, especially the parts related to playing or singing. This is the area of technique. Elasticity, spring, warmth, dryness, tension are all examples of different physiologies. |
| Time and Place of Performance | The time and place beginning from the moment you walk onstage until the final walk off stage. Every performance is contained within a time and place. |

*Figure 2*

The first category is the *Outcome*, which describes what you want to accomplish. Sally wanted *to prepare her schedules*, Barbara wanted *to play Mozart scales with exuberance*. These are examples of outcomes. Notice that they are generally preceded with the infinitive *to*. From the Action/Outcome Grid, you saw that you could have many outcomes for a performance.

*Beliefs*, the second category, describe the attitudes about what seems possible for you to accomplish — what seems pie-in-the-sky versus what seems realistically achievable. Your beliefs also describe what you find meaningful, what you find worthwhile about your outcome — for yourself, the people close to you, and your audience. Your beliefs also describe the kind of person you think will achieve your outcome.

*Values* describe the qualities you find important about your outcome, what you connect to, derive satisfaction from, or feel motivated to fulfill.

*Emotions* are yet another dimension of your inner condition. In this book, we will consider the emotions that best support your outcome, which can differ from the emotions you want to express in the music.

*State of Mind* describes your concentration, your attention, your perception of the environment and inner experiences.

*Physiology*, still another dimension of your inner state, constitutes all the qualities of your muscles, including how they are trained, which includes your technique.

A performer's inner experience of the performance can be thought of as a package of unique outcomes, beliefs, values, emotions, states of mind, and physiologies: every performer will perform with some combination of them. The basic idea of refining your outcomes is to tune each of these qualities so that they all support each other. In other words, after your performance work, you want to know what you want (outcome); believe it is possible, meaningful to you, your

Breaking down your inner experience into these categories is simply one way to isolate distinctions in an otherwise seamless experience. A change in one will affect a change in the others, as they all overlap.

support people, and the audience, and identify with the kind of person who could and would perform that way (beliefs); value your performing (values); feel the emotions that will enrich and encourage attaining your outcome (emotions); adjust your concentration, imagination, or focus until it is just right (state of mind); tune up your muscles until you can execute your outcomes (physiology), and bring it all into the performance.

Top performers will refine the qualities from each category and "tune" them so that they all work together. Poor performers typically will not. For example, look at figure 3 and compare Performer A and Performer B. Performer A has distinguished his outcomes, beliefs, values, emotions, states of mind, and physiology. Each one is vivid, rich, and distinct. Most importantly, though, each supports the other. Performer B has not distinguished any of these parts of his inner experience. His vague, dull, muffled experiences do not work together.

We know intuitively that Performer A will most certainly give a good performance and Performer B will not, even though their skill level or their music is not known. Notice, too, the bottom line: they both will take their package of outcomes, beliefs, emotions, values, state of mind, and physiology into the time and place of the performance, regardless of its condition.

A professional can refine the qualities in these distinct categories and, like a collage artist, "cut and paste" them to create different internal experiences. A powerful performer, for example, might combine a refined sense of austerity (emotion) with a delicate sense of ease (physiology) and a rarefied, musical slip of imagination (state of mind) — all on the turn of a phrase — and produce a sound that will send chills down a listener's spine. Then, a few measures later, this same artist might transform her inner experience into a soaring sense of awe (emotion), a large pulsing feeling in her muscles (physiology), and an attitude where twenty or thirty images reel

| Performer A | Performer B |
|---|---|
| Has a vivid, potent, and compelling representation of what he wants in a performance — the quality, the sounds, the feelings — and it is so desirous it makes his mouth water. | Has a vague idea of what he wants in a performance. Certainly wants to please, but is not quite sure whom (the audience, himself, his teacher?) Vaguely wants this performance to be "good." |
| Believes this kind of performance is *possible* for him and that it can be *meaningful* to himself, his immediate support group, and also to the audience. Also feels he is the kind of person who *could* and *would* perform this way. | Believes his outcome is *sort of* possible. Hasn't considered how performing this way would be meaningful to himself or the audience. Believes he probably *could* perform this way, but he is not the kind of person who *would*. |
| *Values* this kind of performing, believes it is very important. Would miss performing this way deeply if he didn't do it. | Doesn't value performing this way as much as visiting friends, getting a steady job, or earning a lot of money, for example. |
| Has the appropriate *physiology* to carry out his representation of what he wants in performing. (A state of nimbleness, warmth, and elasticity in his skin and muscles, for example.) | Works to not be nervous. Basically tries to not shake or sweat or get dry mouth. |
| Has the appropriate *emotion* for what he wants in this performance (excitement, humor, perhaps, or calmness, seriousness, altruism) and feels it richly. | Tries to keep the emotion of calmness, but it keeps flaring up into anxiety at the thought of performing. |
| Has a *state of mind* that organizes the whole experience so it can happen fluidly inside the performer (as opposed to a state of mind with a steady, interrupting internal voice). | Keeps talking to himself about what is coming up, evaluating what happened, reminding himself about his teacher's admonitions, perhaps even hearing his teacher's or the audience's possible criticisms at different points in the music. |
| Brings all of the above with him *to the time and place of performing*. | Brings all of the above with him *to the time and place of performing*. |

The
Bottom
Line

*Figure 3*

through her imagination (state of mind), creating an excitement that grips the audience and doesn't let go. These adjustments in her inner experience underlie the nuances in her musical expression. The sheer skill and sophisticated flexibility to isolate, refine, and combine qualities from these categories is what performance artistry is all about.

You already have many different values, or physiologies, or emotions. You can pick and choose among them and put them together in different combinations, and each combination will create a unique experience. You can learn to make these adjustments and acquire the flexibility to create a broad range of distinct experiences: your expressiveness will certainly broaden as a result.

In this chapter, we will continue to examine the first and most important category, *outcomes*. Then, in the next chapter, we will look at each of the remaining categories — beliefs, values, emotions, physiology, and state of mind — and outline how you can refine and expand your outcomes with them.

## Outcomes

Outcomes spearhead your inner state. They need to be sharp, strong, and finely tuned to give you a clear idea of where you're headed and what qualities you need to get there. Consider Performer B's vague *sort of wanting to play well*. How could he possibly develop a refined emotion to support that? How well could he possibly stimulate a distinct physiology to support *sort of wanting to play well*? Without clearly knowing what he is trying to accomplish, he will find it difficult to get his inner experience together. He will need to develop, refine, and enrich what he wants before he can shape any inner experience at all, to say nothing of one that is conflict-free, compelling, and rich.

Fortunately, even a vague notion of "playing well" can be guided through the *Four Procedures* and *Tuning Questions* listed below, which are like stations along an assembly line, and the end product will be a well-built concept.

In the following discussions, I will describe how a student from a master class, Laura, began forming her outcomes using these four procedures.

### Four Procedures to Refine an Outcome

Laura loved music, but hated to practice. She said she *didn't want to feel like she had to drag herself into the practice room*. She hated the heavy feeling and the feeling that she was being pushed. The whole idea of practicing was undesirable. She knew what she didn't want — which is the negative form of knowing what she wanted.

So I asked her what she wanted instead of *feeling like she had to drag herself into the practice room*. What would she have if she didn't have those feelings? After a few moments of searching, she said she wanted *to enjoy practicing*. Her answer was a description of what she wants, rather than what she doesn't want. Though a simple change, we can now begin to refine her outcome.

Other examples of outcomes stated in the negative are: I don't want to shake during the performance; I don't want to have a memory slip; I don't want to make a fool of myself; I don't want to tense up.

To change the negative form to the positive, ask yourself "If I weren't shaking during the performance, what would I want to feel instead?" By asking this kind of question, you will be able to focus on your target and can begin to refine what you want. Instead of shaking you may want *to feel ease, distinguished with a sense of elasticity,*

1

Make sure that what you want is in the positive form.

"I don't want to
miss the high note"
becomes "I want to
sing the high
note_____ (in a
particular way)."

perhaps. Or perhaps you would like *to feel solidness and strength.* In any case, the question will cause you to define the quality you are pursuing, which will then lead the way toward invoking it. You won't be stuck with what you don't want.

This concept is not the same as thinking positive thoughts over and over. Drumming positive statements to yourself may do something, but it is unlikely that this approach will quench your concerns about your performance. When there is something that you don't want related to your performance, it is extremely important to address and satisfy that concern completely. "I don't want to miss the high note," for example, might suggest that you have not adequately learned to hit the high note. You should then develop what you need to hit the high note. Your concern should be treated as a signal to direct you toward the appropriate work, since your work as a performer is to tend to and satisfy every single concern. A positive thought, like, "I can do it" might help, but it would be irrelevant in directing you to what you need in order to hit the high note with a sense of ease.

Shifting the negative to the positive is just shifting the form of the language and the nature of the emphasis. Keeping the outcome in the negative form, such as *not making a fool of myself*, would be difficult to refine and, perhaps, by emphasizing it, you may end up appearing quite foolish. So, as in this example, it is far better for you to consider what you would want if you were not *making a fool of yourself* — and emphasize that.

## 2

### Make sure that what you want is specific.

Laura's outcome, *to enjoy practicing*, was still vague and could be much more refined. She needed to specify the how, when, where, what, and whys of her outcome to make it more specific. How do you want to enjoy your practicing? What do you want to enjoy practicing? When do you want to enjoy your practicing? Where do you want to enjoy your practicing? Why do you want to enjoy your practicing?

Laura answered these questions with "to enjoy rehearsing 'Un bel di,' from Puccini's *Madama Butterfly* [what] at home [where], regularly [how], early in the mornings during February [when], so that I can learn the aria faster [why]" which is a richer, more complete outcome. Just at the second step, she had progressed a long way from *not wanting to drag herself into the practice room.* The ideas are completely different.

This what-where-how-when-why part of the exercise will help you identify something concrete to represent to yourself and move away from vague ideas. It also helps with the next exercise: Describing your outcome in your different senses.

Generate at least two pictures, two sounds, two feelings of your outcome to make it palpable, then cut and paste them together. Five representations of each is best.

I asked Laura to see what she would see if she were *enjoying practicing "Un bel di," at home, early in the mornings during February, so that she could learn the aria faster.* I asked her what she would hear and what she would feel also, and directed her to piece together what she imagined.

First she imagined the cover of her *Arias for Soprano*, which she said was like a close-up picture, and then imagined another picture of her piano, in the morning light. Next, with a little practice, she *superimposed* the picture of the *Arias for Soprano* on her mental picture of the piano. At this point, they were like two scraps of ideas pasted together.

Next, she practiced feeling an urge to move toward something. Her first few attempts to generate the feeling were not very strong, but she kept practicing until she was able to isolate the distinct feeling of heading toward something and until she could reproduce it easily. The feeling was another scrap from her imagination. She

3

Describe what you want in all of your senses.

repeated this work with the cool feel of February mornings. Now she had two feeling scraps — an urge to move toward something, and the cool feel of February mornings.

Next, she developed the sound of herself saying "Ah, Puccini" in an exquisite, inviting tone and heard the sounds of the opening phrases, clearly, beautifully rendered. Two more scraps from her imagination. At this point, her work consisted of the list below:

*Pictures* = close up of *Arias for Soprano* + full picture of piano in the morning sun of February

*Tactile Sensations* = urge to move toward something + feel of cool February mornings on her feet

*Sounds* = her own inspiring, inviting tone, "Puccini" + the opening phrases of "Un bel di" beautifully rendered, rich in her inner hearing

To put them all together, she practiced combining the two feelings — the urge to move toward something and the cool mornings in February — which, at first, was a little like rubbing her stomach while patting her head. After a few attempts, though, the feelings blended into one feeling, a combination of moving toward something and the cool February mornings. She felt a distinct shift in her feelings when they combined.

Then, at the peak of the new feeling, she pasted in the visual images of the cover and the piano. She rehearsed re-intensifying the feelings and re-intensifying the images at the same time, until the feeling and pictures became one sensation.

Then, like laying a multi-track recording, she dubbed in the sounds, "Puccini" in her exquisite tone, and the opening phrases rendered clearly and beautifully. Again, she systematically re-intensified each scrap of her imagination while simultaneously intensifying the sounds.

She spent a few more moments getting them all together at the same time. Laura admitted that keeping track of these scraps in her imagination was a bit slippery, and recalling, isolating, intensifying, and associating each picture, feeling, and sound required concentrated work, though it only took a few moments.

By deliberately working her imagination this way, Laura began fleshing out her outcome, giving it substance. She crafted her vague notion of *not wanting to drag herself into the practice room* into this much more appealing representation. It was richer and therefore easier to manage and fulfill. These procedures will work with any outcome from the Action/Outcome Grid.

Laura wanted to practice this way to learn the music faster, because she wanted *to live with the aria for a longer time before the performance* — another outcome. She also wanted *to achieve disciplined rehearsal habits as a reflection of herself as an artist* — yet another outcome. Notice that these outcomes fit on the Action/Outcome Grid in the Rehearsal Stage, at different Issue Levels.

Laura imagined these other outcomes and her newly developed outcome simultaneously. They went together very well.

These four procedures are a specific approach to enriching your imagination of what you want in your performing. The skill to cut and paste scraps of your imagination — of your whole experience — is a basic skill

4

Imagine how this outcome fits with some of your other outcomes.

of a performer and you can continue to develop it. Without this skill, you would be stuck with the feelings, pictures, and sounds you have about a performance, whether they are particularly helpful to you or not.

To render every issue on the Action/Outcome Grid using these four procedures may not always be necessary, especially when your outcomes already seem developed to you, but doing so would certainly make the performance compelling.

## Tuning Questions (TQ)

The Tuning Questions are highly useful tools to keep the ideas moving through your "assembly line"; they were developed by Dr. Richard Bandler and Dr. John Grinder to help clear up language usage among professionals. Like tools to keep in your hip pocket, they will help you considerably, while you build your inner state.

TQ1.   Questions to tune Nouns:

   Ask *What*? or *Which*? or *Who*, specifically?

   *Example:*

   Statement:      I want to play exciting music.
   Response:       *What* exciting music, specifically?

   Statement:      The critics won't like the
                   performance.
   Response:       *Which* critics, specifically, won't like
                   the performance?

TQ2.   Question to tune Verbs:

   Ask *How*, specifically?

   *Example:*

   Statement:      I want to create something for the
                   audience.
   *Response:*     *How*, specifically, do you want to
                   create something for the audience?

Statement:  I want to learn my music.
Response:   *How*, specifically, do you want to
            learn your music?

TQ3.  Question to tune words like all, never, always,
      everybody, nowhere, everywhere:

      Emphasize the word, and add a questioning
      inflection.

      *Example:*
      Statement:  Everyone thinks it was a bad
                  performance.
      Response:   EVERYONE thinks it was a bad
                  performance?

      Statement:  I will never sing with full, easy
                  resonance.
      Response:   NEVER?

TQ4.  Questions to tune words like should, should not,
      must, must not, have to, cannot, ought to, ought
      not:

      Ask What would happen if you did? (or did not?)
      or What prevents you?

      *Example:*
      Statement:  I must keep my hand position firm.
      Response:   What would happen if you didn't
                  keep your hand position firm?

      Statement:  I have to please my coach.
      Response:   What would happen if you didn't
                  please your coach?

      Statement:  I can't sing the high note.
      Response:   What, specifically, prevents you
                  from singing the high note?

TQ5.  Questions to tune the -er and -est words in the language, such as easier, better, most, faster, greatest:

Ask Better than what (or whom)? or According to what standard?

*Example:*

Statement:  I want to play better.
Response:  Better than what or whom?

Statement:  My technique must be the best.
Response:  The best of whom? According to what standard?

You can use these questions anytime. They will clarify what you are thinking, especially when you get stuck. Sometimes, they may even break open a block you may have had for years.

As an example of these questions in action, listen to my session with Deanna, a pianist who wanted to be a classical performer. She never felt comfortable playing music by Mozart, Bach, or Beethoven, even though she had the skills, desire, and talent to play their works beautifully. When I asked her what prevented her from feeling comfortable (TQ4), she said she didn't feel like she belonged there.

I asked her what prevented her from belonging. (TQ4)

She said, "a feeling."

"What feeling, specifically?" (TQ1)

"The feeling that I am not supposed to be up here playing classical music."

"Playing classical music how, specifically?" (TQ2)

"With finesse ... and authority."

"What would happen if you played classical music with finesse and authority?" (TQ4)

"They would laugh at me, think I was trying to be

pompous."

"Who, specifically would laugh at you?" (TQ1)

"The audience"

"Who in the audience would laugh at you and think you were pompous?" (TQ1)

"Everybody."

"EVERYBODY?" (TQ3)

"Well no, not everybody. The people who know better."

"Which people? Who know *what* better, specifically?" (TQ1)

"The people who are more educated than me ... the ones who know more about ... wait a minute. I have as much ... more training than those people ... than *that* person."

After a few moments, she said "You know what I'm thinking? I'm thinking of my mother–in–law who said I was good at pop music but that I couldn't play classical music *like her niece."*

I could see Deanna's wheels turning. "How specifically would your mother–in–law know better than you about whether you could or should play classical music with finesse and authority?" (QT2)

"She wouldn't ... She doesn't even play the piano."

"What would happen if you played classical music like her niece?" (QT4)

"Nothing. I'd probably enjoy it ... my mother–in–law ... I don't know, but ... so what ... I'd enjoy it."

She was really beaming now.

"Imagine playing Bach now in front of the audience. What is it like?"

After a few moments she said, "It is really comfortable. I used to have this feeling that the audience was thinking awful thoughts about me, like they thought I was a fraud, or was incompetent."

"Yeah, and how would they think those thoughts?" (QT2)

"Of course they are probably just wanting to enjoy

the music. It is funny, now. They'd look funny if they were scheming to think all those awful thoughts. It seems so silly, now."

Deanna had simply connected her thoughts about her mother–in–law with the audience and performing classical music. These Tuning Questions helped move her ideas to what she really wanted — *to play classical music with authority and finesse*. She could now refine this outcome through the procedures above, making it more specific, richer in her imagination, and more comfortable in her overall desires.

Throughout any of the exercises in the rest of the book, keep these questions handy. Use them to tune up your thoughts, sharpen what you mean to yourself, build clearer images, sounds, and feelings.

Once your outcome is developed, you can enrich it even more by adding to it the beliefs, values, emotions, state of mind, and physiology that will best support it. In the next sections, you will examine each of these areas and how to use them to enrich your performances. The final section will help you carry your work into the performance itself.

# IV

## SUPPORTING THE PERFORMANCE

**Beliefs: Possibility, Meaning, Identity**

### Possibility

*Is it **possible** for you or someone like you in a similar situation to achieve your outcome?*

Marilyn, an organist, had agreed to give a special performance for the dedication of a new university organ. Though her performance had been scheduled a year in advance, by the time she came to see me, eleven months had elapsed and she was still not ready to perform. Unprepared, she sat nervously in front of me, just three and a half weeks before the performance. Embarrassed, she said she didn't know why she avoided rehearsing. She was stuck, confused, and full of conflict.

The purpose of this question and the subsequent questions in this chapter is to help you refine your outcome. They are pragmatic questions to ask yourself because you will need to make sure your outcome is 1) possible, 2) meaningful to yourself, your support group, and the audience, and 3) that you are the kind of person who could and would perform this way.

Orient yourself
toward the main
issues in your
performance

I asked her, "When you think of the performance, is there anything desirable about it? Is there something appealing to you? In other words, why not just not perform it?"

She stumbled for a moment and said, "I couldn't just not do it. I've already said I would do it, and besides it's a real break and an honor. I just have been dreading this concert."

"What would have to change if you were to fully look forward to this performance?" I asked. "The music? The people? What is so undesirable? Is it the hall itself, the organ, the rehearsal time, the coming on and off stage?" I was orienting her to the points on the Action/Outcome Grid. The problem would certainly fit within the four stages or issue levels of performing.

We discovered that the main issue was that the sponsor not only chose the music, but insisted on turning the pages for her, setting the organ stops, and arranging various other elements of the performance. He was adamant about the whole matter, and ignored her requests to set her own stops and have her own page turner. Based on her past experiences, she also expected him to try to upstage her, and, because he always behaved so nervously, she felt he would certainly distract her. Under the circumstances, she felt stripped of her power to perform.

Marilyn did not like having this problem and thought she shouldn't even have it in the first place; she thought she should be more professional and adapt to this situation. As it was, though, she could not commit to her performance. She did not even know what she wanted yet. She only knew what she didn't want — a performance she felt helpless about and at the mercy of someone else's control. Thinking she shouldn't have the problem certainly wouldn't resolve it.

The sponsor's insistence had actually undermined her whole approach to performing. Marilyn was used to stimulating her artistic juices, working her imagination, and building her performance during her process of choosing her stops. Without playing with the stops, experimenting with the different timbres, she had nothing to engage her, no starting gate to enter the race. Her frustration and hesitation made sense — she could not have performed well under the circumstances because the issue was not satisfied. Notice that the issues *turning the pages* and *setting the organ stops* fit on the Grid under Parts of the Parts, primarily during the Performing Stage. They also affected the larger issue of Musician, whether she was maintaining her identity as an adaptable professional who could pull it all together or not.

We began the procedures for building an outcome and turned what she didn't want — to feel helpless — into what she wanted: *to feel plugged in and in command of her performance, even with the sponsor turning pages.* In addition, she wanted *to give the audience something, even if it wasn't technically perfect.*

We pulled out the Tuning Questions, such as *to command what, specifically, and how?* She wanted to command her inner feelings, even though the sponsor was nearby, nervous, and turning her pages. She wanted to connect with the music, to command her involvement. She didn't have to be the star; it was his new organ, anyway.

I asked her to get her creative juices flowing, to come up with some ways she could have command of these things even while the sponsor fluttered around her. I directed her attention to find times she was absorbed, even in distracting situations. She hit upon the ideas of reading while around children, while on the train, and while on the bus — all instances where she was in control of her concentration.

What were those times like? Could they be useful in this performance situation? Could she imagine connecting with the music in the same way that she connected with her reading in these other situations? Would it give her just the right kind of command of her involvement?

Orient yourself to what you do want.

Search anywhere in your personal experience for what works.

Is it possible?

Marilyn decided this approach could help, if it were modified, if she "felt" musical; she could adapt it, feel musical and concentrated at the same time; it was different, but it would work and she could get what she wanted. With a little more exploring, we refined these ideas and made sure they would work using the techniques in the chapter titled Artistic Grit, which you will read later in this book.

Once Marilyn was satisfied that she could command her inner state, we began developing her second outcome: *to at least give the audience something, even if the performance wasn't perfect technically.* With only three weeks to go, it seemed like a reasonable outcome. Using the exercises to build her outcome and the Tuning Questions from the previous chapter, we strengthened the idea into a potent outcome, which visibly pleased her. Her face lit up and she relaxed her posture. When you begin to work toward an outcome that is right for you, you, too, may notice a release of tension in your muscles and a warmth in your face. You will certainly experience a signal that it is right.

Then I asked Marilyn *if it was possible for her or someone like her in a similar situation to give the audience something, even if the performance wasn't technically perfect.*

"No," she said suddenly, losing all the color from her face; she slumped in her chair.

As long as it did not seem possible to her, *it was not possible.* Once again, I pulled out the Tuning Questions and "tuned" her answer.

"What prevents it from being possible?" (TQ#4)

"There is not enough time."

"You mean there is NO WAY in the world ANYBODY, ANYWHERE could *give the audience something even if the performance wasn't technically perfect,* in three and a half weeks, with this music?" I asked incredulously (TQ#3).

"Well, if they worked *passionately,*" she blurted out as though it was obvious. "If they were maniacal, kept at it like a fiend," she added.

Under her words lay the idea of how it could actually be *possible* to achieve her outcome. It was the piece she needed to shift her outcome from impossible to possible. It was an understanding, a distinct scrap of her imagination that, once developed, could be "pasted in" to her outcome.

I asked her to examine her idea of *working passionately*. What did *working passionately* look like? What did it feel like? What did it sound like? What would she be doing? She needed to refine and enrich it. As she intensified the quality inside her, it became clearer, stronger, and quite desirable to her. She began to assume an empowered posture: her head was inclined, her breathing became more diaphragmatic.

Next, I asked Marilyn to recall her original images of *giving the audience something even if it wasn't technically perfect* and merge them with her current feelings.

When she combined them, the outcome of *giving the audience something* became synonymous with *working passionately*. They crossed their partitions and became part of the same idea, shifting her outcome from an impossible fantasy to a very real possibility. If she had not added *working passionately* to her outcome, she would have seen the outcome as something desirable, but unlikely. She would not have been able to commit one hundred percent to an outcome that she did not believe was possible.

Notice that *working passionately* was her personal understanding of what she needed. I might have had some other idea of what would make her outcome possible, but it may not have matched her particular desire. There was no need for me to question her choice because whatever representation she brought up was the piece of the puzzle she needed. Now her outcome and how it might be possible could begin to make sense to her.

In the rest of this chapter, I will describe how Marilyn and I continue to draw the qualities from within her that will support her outcome, *to give the audience*

Savour, explore, intensify the distinctive qualities you need or desire to perform.

Merge your outcome with the possibility of it.

Benedict Spinoza

*So long as a man imagines that he cannot do this or that, so long is he determined not to do it; and consequently, so long it is impossible to him that he should do it.*

Is it meaningful
to you to
perform?

When you are going
through these
questions preparing
for your performance,
you may find it
helpful to work with
a pencil and paper. A
few words to jog your
memory will help
unclutter your mind
so that it is freer to
concentrate on
experiencing each of
your images.

*something, even if it is not technically perfect.* She will answer each question with her own chosen quality, such as *working passionately,* which she will experience within herself. Then she will overlap her outcome with the special quality she is experiencing, very much like the cut and paste exercise described in the previous chapter, and intensify them both until the qualities and the outcome fully associate.

## Meaningful to Ourselves

*How would it be personally meaningful for you or someone like you in a similar situation to achieve your outcome?*

Marilyn's response to the question above was immediate. Given the circumstances, she could imagine feeling that she will have *grown as an artist* if she pulled off this performance so that the audience got something, even without technical perfection.

To continue building her inner state, she clarified the images, feelings, and sounds of *growing as an artist* and added them to her outcome. *Giving the audience something, working passionately,* and *growing as an artist* then all became part of the same idea.

For your performances, you will want to perceive the significance of your outcome, and to associate the significance with the outcome itself. In other words, after you ask yourself the above question, then, when you form an answer, add it to the outcome. Connect them until they are one and the same.

*Meaningful to the People Closest to Us*

*How could achieving this outcome be meaningful for the people closest to you or someone like you in a similar situation ?*

Marilyn is very close to her mother, her main support. She could easily imagine her mother's face, beaming with pride about Marilyn's *growing as an artist, becoming more professional.* As she thought of involving herself in such passionate, committed work for so many days, she could see her mother's discrete, supporting glances unobtrusively appearing in the background. The feelings they brought were a welcome, comforting addition to her outcome.

When she thought of her teacher, her other main support, she had to work a little bit harder. At first she could only imagine her teacher scowling at her for waiting so long to prepare and for not being technically perfect. She heard her teacher saying "Well, if you hadn't put it off, then you could have played even better." It was an image that had, in fact, steadily intensified over the last three months.

Because of the work we had done by this point, however, Marilyn's idea of the performance now had become so compelling that it kept popping up, and it was difficult to keep the image of her teacher scowling at her. She remembered other times when her teacher responded much like her mother, proud and pleased at having been part of her learning. Instead of hearing harsh criticism, she imagined her teacher saying,"The sooner you resolve your conflicts and prepare what you want to accomplish in a performance, the better off you will be." She saw her teacher drawing satisfaction and a sense of connection to

Is it meaningful to the people you are closest to?

Combine it with
the outcome.

Marilyn as she got it together. Though Marilyn couldn't really know how her teacher would react, by imagining how her teacher *could* react, she freed herself from the doom and gloom of the other images. As it turned out, her teacher was quite proud of her.

Had Marilyn stepped into the performance with an image of her teacher scowling at her, it probably would have caused a conflict. She might have spent her time on stage feeling guilty, striving to conciliate the image and dissipate the bad feelings, and, at the least, she would not have been able to commit one hundred percent to her performance.

Just as in the previous exercises, Marilyn appropriately placed the supporting images of her mother and teacher with her outcome, which was now a composite of *giving the audience something, working passionately,* and *growing artistically.*

Your spouse, family, teachers, friends, other musicians, especially those on stage with you, are all important people to include in your planning. By imagining how your outcome can benefit the people you are close to, you can pre-empt conflicts. And sensing how they too will derive value will make it easier to commit to your outcome.

Sometimes you may find that if you perform with your outcome, it will actually interfere with someone close to you and threaten his or her support. It can happen with jealous teachers or friends or spouses. This type of conflict often happens with professional concert artists, whose lives become swallowed up by their work. Use the Tuning Questions to clarify your experiences. You may need to modify your outcome. If you cannot sense how what you are committing to could be meaningful to the people close to you, it could become the source of a conflict and therefore be detrimental to your performance.

*Meaningful to the Audience*

*How would or could it be meaningful to the audience for you or someone like you in a similar situation to achieve this outcome?*

Marilyn could see rather easily how *performing so that the audience would get something special* would be meaningful to the audience. Her sense of what the audience would get was beyond words, but she saw it in images of their expressions. She also imagined being a member of the audience feeling the effect of her performing that way, and it was gratifying. She tucked these feelings in with the rest of her ideas.

Some performers, on the other hand, have no idea how their performance could or would benefit the audience. Sometimes, they imagine a hostile, criticizing audience instead. They vividly see how what they are attempting will be *meaningless!* They clearly imagine the audience not responding to them. They remind themselves of how meaningless their performance will be to the audience even as they rehearse, during the performance, and after the performance. They expend energy building up what they don't want rather than what they want. How committed can they be to their performance?

No one can know exactly how an audience will respond, but if you conceive of how they *could* respond with a sense of meaning, it will help you commit more to your performance.

Many performers debate whether an artist should try to please the audience or himself; these arguments concern maintaining artistic integrity versus selling out, and are different from what I am proposing here. You may know that what you want is not what the audience ex-

Is it meaningful to the audience for you to perform?

pects, or wants, but you can still imagine how your outcome could be meaningful to them. Your outcomes may surprise, enrich, or stimulate your audience. Connecting the meaning that the audience could derive from your performance to your outcome will only make it richer and more compelling.

*Identifying with the Performance*

**Who could do this?**
**Is this me?**

*What kind of person could and would perform with this outcome?*

In response to this question, Marilyn imagined a portrait of a woman with courage, fortitude, passion, and self-acceptance. She was the kind of woman who learned from her mistakes, glided over them, and reformed her attention with interest. All of the qualities emerged from the essence of this woman's expression.

*When were you like that kind of person, at least partially?*

In response to this question, a portrait of herself with these qualities emerged from a collection of memories: when her car broke down on the freeway, when she failed a major exam in school, when her student loan money in college didn't come in. These were all instances where she managed herself beautifully, even in hardship and disappointment.

The two portraits hung in her mind side by side, and, as she noticed the similarities, the image of herself began naturally to merge with the image of the kind of woman who could and would perform with these outcomes, forming a large, beautiful, genuine rendering of herself. When she added the portrait to the rest of her ideas, it permeated them. She said she lost sight of the image, but knew it was there, coloring the performance with those qualities.

Now, her outcome was a rich composite of giving the audience something, working passionately, growing as an artist, feeling the pride of her mother and teacher, sensing the appreciation of the audience, and feeling her courage, fortitude, passion, and ability to learn from her mistakes. As all these images, feelings, and sounds blended, they created an inner experience that was unique, more than just the sum of the parts, and the overall effect was very compelling to her.

When you form your outcome, you want to identify with it completely. Marilyn Horne, Tina Turner, The Grateful Dead all have different ideas of performing, but they each fully identify with their own. Not identifying with the performance, having a subtle feeling that *this isn't the real me*, is enough to interfere with complete commitment.

It requires work to sit down and ask yourself these questions; but this is the work of performers, because it affects your internal state. Packing together desirable answers to these questions will turn your performance into something desirable. You will feel better about it, be able to respond better to it, and more able to develop and benefit from a compelling internal condition. Marilyn certainly did. Her vision of feeling helpless, which delayed her rehearsing, was now transforming into a beautiful vision of her achieving something possible, meaningful, and something she could identify with. It was becoming quite desirable to her.

Adjust anything about the performance until you find complete identification.

Is it valuable to
you to perform?

## Values: Connecting with the Performance

*What are three different values you enjoy seeing, feeling, or
hearing about?*

I suggested that Marilyn consider a wide range of
events, even outside of music, to respond to this question.
As an additional guideline, I asked her to think of what
she cared about, what was important to her.

She scanned through her ideas until she finally hit
upon *people working together. People working together*
generated a strong, attractive feeling and, when her image
became clearer, I could see her facial expression become
more relaxed. I encouraged Marilyn to imagine being part
of *people working together*, to feel the feelings, see what she
would see, and to hear what she would hear as if she were
experiencing this, deriving the full value. As she pondered
and elaborated on *people working together*, she began to
visibly glow.

By this time, she had the hang of shaping these
individual inner qualities in response to these questions,
enriching them, and manipulating them, so it was easy for
her to infuse her ideas of performing with this inner
experience of value. Once again, Marilyn's presence
delicately illuminated. Her vocal tone deepened and the
core of her voice resonated distinctly. Her eyes even
seemed clearer. When you adjust your inner experiences
toward those qualities that you admire, your outer
appearance will alter, too, even if you are unaware of it.

Marilyn commented that after adding the feeling
of *people working together,* the emphasis had shifted among
her ideas of performing. It was now not just a matter of
making the performance work or learning a professional
lesson, it was something that would be *valuable*. The
cluster of distinct ideas now seemed to have a pattern. The
performance felt more whole. The value had solidified her
idea of performing.

Dr. Herbert Benson, Associate Professor of Medicine at The Harvard Medical School and Director of Hypertension Section of Boston's Beth Israel Hospital, developed a research program for athletes that studied the effects of associating *religious values* with the performance of athletes.

Dr. Benson instructed his patients to develop an experience of their religious values in a similar way Marilyn developed her sense of *people working together*. On a daily basis, the patients were to deliberately conjure their religious feeling. At the height of their religious feeling, they were to say to themselves a cue word, like a mantra in meditation, that would, like a trigger button, later help them re-experience the religious value.

He wired them with heart, blood-pressure, temperature, and other physiological monitors and tested them walking and running on a treadmill in their ordinary state. Then he instructed them to repeat their cue word to trigger their deep religious feeling while they were walking and running and he re-tested them to discover whether his patients physiology would change.

The changes were astounding: the athletes' blood pressure, heart rate, and metabolism all performed more efficiently. To illustrate the results, one of his patients was filmed running around the track before and after this interposing of religious values. The different runs, seen side by side, in slow motion, showed that the first run was stiff, jerky, and full of unnecessary movements and the second run, by comparison, was fluid, full of gliding, *efficient* movements. In the second run, the runner looked like a different man, lean, sleek, agile, focused.

Notice that an athletic activity like running is not by itself religious. But by associating a deep religious experience with the activity, it *becomes* religious, in the sense that it brings along the physiological characteristics of their religious experience *into the activity* (lower heart pulse rates, reduced tensions, smoother muscular efficiency, etc). By developing a deep religious feeling

As Dr. Frank Wilson, a neurologist, points out, muscular functioning is the same for both athletes and musicians at the neurological level. The difference is the choice of muscles — athletes basically develop the limbs and torso, musicians, the fine muscles of the hands, throat and lip area.

Explore your values.

What do you value that will help you get things done?

beforehand and then associating it with the activity, the athletes changed their physiological functioning, which directly improved their performance.

Dr. Benson's work demonstrates that performers can pre-condition themselves and carry that condition into their activity, and it will affect their performance. This pre-conditioning is what I am calling performance work, as opposed to other kinds of music learning. However, cultivating the singular quality of religious value, its serenity and meditative distinctiveness, is only one choice. It will have its unique effect on the performance. But, from an artistic point of view, a performer needs a wide choice of inner conditions, built from any number of other values, even other qualities of the human experience, like beliefs, or emotions, or states of mind, and they will all affect the performance in their unique ways.

Marilyn chose *people working together*. A deep religious feeling may not have meant as much to her, and the serenity may have not fueled her fire to meet her enormous task. *People working together* had an engaging quality she needed. It was not too overpowering, so it did not interfere with her ideas of working passionately. It fit her outcome especially well and suited her personally.

Dr. David McClelland of Harvard separated human values into three basic categories — power, affiliation, and achievement — and Dr. Genie Labourde separated them into similar groups — potency, connectedness, and identity. You can use these groupings to stimulate your sense of values. As you read through the list, think of your rehearsing and performing and let the words stimulate the qualities you may want to develop and infuse into your performing.

*Potency* refers to your ability to accomplish something. Your values about potency reflect the qualities that you believe are necessary to get things done. Organization, hard-work, flexibility, naturalness, creativity, power, status, intelligence are all examples of qualities you may value relative to potency.

*Connectedness* refers to belonging to other people. You value what you think will keep you connected. These values include love, family, honor, unselfishness, friendliness, honesty, and religion.

*Identity* refers to the qualities of who you think you are. The values of identity are those qualities which you think will maintain your identity. Personal honor, creativity, character, generosity, and integrity are some examples.

Pick any of these or generate your own list. An activity or situation that expresses the value is sometimes easier to grasp than an abstract value. Seeing children playing together, or expressions of joy on people's faces, or awards being handed out are examples of what may stimulate a sense of value in you. Marilyn could easily identify *people working together*, and by imagining it fully, she was able to draw out what was valuable to her. The value was a certain quality of experience, rather than a particular word.

By associating a deep sense of value with your performance, you can connect with it more easily. The value will change your feelings — even your physiology, as Dr. Benson demonstrated. You may find that you approach the performance differently, think of it differently, act and rehearse differently; in the end, it will suit you better.

> What do you value that will help you connect with people?
>
> What do you value that will help you maintain your identity?
>
> Associate your values with your work.

## Emotions

*What emotion would best support your outcome?*
*If I feel _____ in preparing this outcome, how would it affect my performance?*

Marilyn experimented with several different emotions to find the best emotion to support her outcome. She tried *determined*, but it seemed too harsh, too narrow an

What feels
right?

Does the emotion
fit the outcome?

emotion for the way her approach to the performance was shaping up. Next she tried *courageous*, and it fit better, but not quite perfectly. She cycled through several other emotions, including *compassion, freedom, joy, awe, love, responsibility,* and *hope.*

Though none of these fit exactly, just going through the exercise helped fill out her ideas because each emotion conjured a unique aspect of the outcome. Feeling *determined*, she thought of several ways she could arrange her schedule, knock out distractions, and insist on practice time from the people around her. Feeling *compassion,* she could imagine encouraging herself under the intense time pressure, freeing her to keep working. Feeling *love,* she felt light and could imagine the day sailing by, making the work easier to manage. In the end, she selected an emotion that was somewhere between *courage* and *joy.* She tuned this emotion in her inner feeling and maintained it while she brought in all of her other feelings. It flavored her whole attitude toward the performance with its distinctiveness.

When you select an emotion, make sure it *will* support your outcome. Some emotions will be too intense for your outcome, others too light. Some won't fit with what you are comfortable bringing to the audience. For Marilyn, the emotion between courage and joy gave her enough of the commitment and enough of the lightness to endure the pressure of preparing this performance. Even though she needed *passion* to fulfill her outcome, an underlying courage and joy would tie the whole experience together, enabling her to enter and exit her passionate work with greater ease.

In order to generate a wider range of emotions to interpret the music, Joan Wall, professor of music at Texas Woman's University, uses an effective technique in her performance classes. The performers select three different emotions, one contrasting the other two. Then someone in the audience calls out the three different emotions at random times during the performance. The performer tries to recreate the emotion on demand.

As an example, the performer may choose *love, excitement*, and *fear* — two similar and one contrasting emotion. The performer begins his performance feeling *love*. Then, during the performance, the audience member calls out *fear* and the performer changes his emotion to *fear*. After a while, the audience member calls out *excitement*, and so on. The effect is that the performer gets both flexibility and new ideas about interpreting the music, and the performances nearly always end up more interesting.

## State of Mind

*What state of mind would best support your outcomes?*

This question is an important one and sometimes trickier to answer than any of the others. Concentration and creativity are examples of states of mind, and we are not always concentrated, nor always creative. With different states of mind, we are in them and out of them at different times. The state of mind is how we think of things, the arrangement and traffic of thinking. A *musical state of mind* , for example, tips our thoughts to hear the fresh moment-by-moment unfolding of the phrases, the character of the harmonies, the expectation, the magic, the flow of musical ideas as they occur. We don't always slip into a musical state, and the music may seem dry.

"The music?" Marilyn asked. "To think musically, is that a state of mind?"

"Yes, " I replied. "It is when your imagination slips into a musical gear, when it is easy to imagine the music richly. Have you ever been in a state like that, that was special, and the music seemed to flow?"

"Yes. Like when the focus is on the music, yet not on the music, on the flow, the connection. Like when the

How is your thinking?

HERBERT BENSON

*In tennis parlance,
a game played at a
high level of
winning expertise
is often said to be
played "in the
zone."...the zone
involves a mental
state  so complete
and intense that it
evokes a state of
almost
semiconscious
euphoria—one
that...enables a top
player to achieve
his or her peak
performance.*

music seems to expand, like moving the orchestra into the middle of your being?" Marilyn's posture had begun to shift, to gain fluidity. You may notice your own body attitude become looser as you concentrate on a state of mind.

*When were the last three times you were in that state of mind?*

"If you were to recall the last couple of times you felt that way and let yourself slip into the memory, right now, do you think it would support you in *giving the audience something*, with all of the qualities you have developed so far?" I asked.

"Yes, it would. It would give me the music, if you know what I mean," Marilyn responded.

"Once again, re-imagine those times, and just as you did with the other qualities, let yourself slip all the way into that state of mind. You want to get the best of it. Go all the way into it, just long enough to get it, your whole thinking."

She took a deep breath. Her skin reddened slightly, and her eyebrows lifted. Then, suddenly, a beatific expression filled her face. This was a cue that she had succeeded in entering a new state of mind.

"Yes, " I almost whispered. "In the most appropriate way, pull up your other ideas about the performance."

Her face paled slightly again; her breath paused, suspended for a couple of seconds. Then she took another deep breath, and slowly the beatific expression emerged, and remained.

"How is that?" I murmured. She was luxuriating in the sensation.

"It's wonderful," Marilyn reported. "It brings the music ... I know that doesn't make much sense, but it's like I can hear the music easier somehow."

Slipping into another state of mind needs special care, because it means completely leaving the state of mind that you are in while you are doing the work. It requires a knack of forgetting and imagining, and remembering later, of shuffling around. You need to set it up ahead of time to organize the two procedures — slipping into the state of mind and merging it with the outcome.

Some musicians say, "I want to get all the way into the music," but they feel resistances to moving into this other state of mind. Usually, this signals their fear that giving up to another, particularly involving state of mind will be a loss of control that they are not sure they will be able to get back. Concerns can be anything. "But I don't want to make a fool of myself," or "What if there is a fire?" or "What if I get so involved I forget the music?" are examples of concerns that can keep you in your current state of mind.

Dr. John Grinder, a language and communications expert, points out that top performers cope with this phenomena by arranging "lifelines." In other words, they arrange a set of conditions — ties to reality — that will enable them to slip into peak states of mind and come out of them again at the appropriate time. That they arrange this ahead of time is what differentiates them from other performers. Even the best performers would interrupt themselves if they didn't take the time to arrange the appropriate conditions for them to completely involve themselves in the music.

To arrange these conditions is a matter of searching out every concern about slipping into a different state of mind, and making sure each concern is addressed appropriately — that is, with lifelines that can safely pull you back, even when drifting into the stratosphere of your imagination. Dealing with concerns, objections, interruptions, and hesitations will be covered in the chapter titled Artistic Grit.

CHRIS EVERT LLOYD
*I've had matches where everything has gone right. You play in the zone, over your head where everything is like a dream. When you play matches like that, you want to play more.*

Use each of your concerns to guide you to build a secure safety net, so that you *can* freely commit 100%.

Involving your
body.

## Physiology: The Body State

*What physiology (body state) would best support your outcome?*

Like states of mind, body states are distinct. The choices of what you can feel are endless, and the wider your pallet, the better off you will be. Instead of choosing grossly between tension and relaxation, you will be able to select, refine, and combine every shade in between. You could perform a phrase of music with a buoyant feeling in your body, and you would have quite a different result if you performed that phrase with a solid feeling in your body. Your body could be buoyant, pert, frisky, spry, agile, stiff, solid, firm, compact, dense, languid, numb, springy, cool, hot, and each of these will result in a different quality. Any and all of them could be useful. I asked Marilyn to think about the physiology that would support her outcome.

"I am really not used to this," she objected.

"Let's stand up," I invited. "Let's choose a feeling of springiness, just to start somewhere. Give yourself a little time to find the feeling of spring in your muscles. You may want to stretch out. Put aside any other considerations of the performance. Just move a little until you feel a springiness in your muscles."

Marilyn stood up and began stretching her arms, spreading her fingers in front of her. After a few minutes of shaking her feet, bending, turning, breathing deep breaths, she finally arrived at a springy feeling in her muscles.

The next question is whether or not a particular body state will support your outcomes for a particular performance.

"While you keep that feeling, " I advised Marilyn, "imagine *giving the audience something*, just enough to evaluate whether this feeling in your body will support you."

Though it was nice, and felt good, Marilyn thought this sensation was somehow too frivolous. She liked the animation in the springiness, but wanted more direction, more drive, more sweat, perhaps. She wanted to feel warm, but agile, a more solid feeling perhaps.

Her imagination was working. She continued to explore for her right feeling. At one point, she headed for "relaxation," but after experimenting with it, she tossed it out for not having enough "juice" in it. She continued exploring her body states until she isolated one that was firm, yet agile and highly animated, and viscous (thick). In order to locate and keep track of the individual feeling she wanted, she found a way to hang her arms in the air as though they were balancing on an up-blowing current of air, and to lean forward, as though she were about to take a step. This body position felt to Marilyn like it fostered the particular quality she wanted.

Will this body state support your outcome?

She practiced getting in and out of this body state, using this posture as a handle. Then, once she was able to easily recall the particular feeling, she pulled up her outcome — all the ideas she had built and combined up to this point — and pasted them one at a time into this firm, agile, highly animated, viscous feeling.

Engage the outcome with the body state.

For example, just as she felt the *emotion* between courage and joy flooding her body, she floated her arms in the air, and leaned forward, kicking in the firm, agile, animated, viscous feeling. When she re-experienced *working passionately*, she again found the feeling in her body. She cycled through all of her ideas until her entire "vision" of the performance engaged this distinct feeling in her muscles.

Janet Bookspan, in coaching opera singers, will sometimes ask the singer to imagine the "heartbeat" of the character. She instructs the singer to walk around the piano, in the pace and style —the heartbeat — of the character, until the walk is distinct. Then, the singer, while

The Alexander Technique, The Jacques-Dalcroze Method, The Feldenkrais Method, areobics, special diets, and other programs are various approaches to creating and refining specified physical states. The important aspect to realize is that your body has within it a vast number of qualities that you can isolate and refine: those you choose will affect your performance. Rather than limt yourself and choose certain body states as the "correct" states, you can choose the states that support your outcomes. The wider your palette of choices, the more you can support a richer expressiveness.

keeping the same physiology of the walk, will immediately begin singing while gliding into a stance. This technique is highly effective, and as a standard rehearsal technique, will help you involve your physiology.

Claudio Arrau says that his fluid piano technique is based on feeling his muscles moving like a cat's. His description suggests a physiology that has confident spring and quick-stretch, with a completely relaxed follow-through to every movement. Isolating, refining a particular state into your muscles while you are playing will have a dramatic impact on your technique.

Every quality of expressiveness will have a distinctive, underlying physiological profile. All of your work as a performer is aimed at creating the optimum physiology to execute the performance. Your outcomes, beliefs, values, emotions, state of mind will all affect your physiology, some more dramatically than others.

Your aim is to introduce fluid shifts in your physiology. In fact, one way to view your performance is as an exquisitely choreographed stream of distinctive, subtle physiologies that create the expressiveness and execution of your performance.

Once you merge your outcome with beliefs, values, emotions, a state of mind, and a body state that supports that outcome, you need to imagine these elements combining with the performance's time and place.

## Time and Place of the Performance

*What will you see, hear, and feel that will signal the time and place of the performance?*

Marilyn knew quite a bit about the time and place of her performance, which was scheduled in a college auditorium, on an open, exposed stage. The walls of the stage were lined with large wood panels, all lightly stained, which continued out and up from the stage and along the walls beside the audience seats. The organ pulled out from a section of the wall and could be rolled to almost any spot on the stage. A spotlight, two side lights, and a row of hanging lights would illuminate the stage. One bright light would shine down on Marilyn's music from straight above. The stage entrance was through a door made of a wall panel; backstage was dark. The greenroom, with one mirrored wall, was lit with ceiling-mounted fluorescent tubes. Marilyn would need to come already dressed to the performance.

The time of the performance was 3:00 p.m., Sunday afternoon.

I explained to Marilyn a simple, yet effective technique to take her state with her into the performance. I commented that she would *see* certain elements — the lighting, the color of the wood, the organ keys, the peculiar light on the stage, the brilliant light on the music, the notes of the music, the change from the greenroom fluorescent light, to the backstage darkness, to the brilliance on stage as she prepares to go on.

She would also *hear* certain things — the creak in the door, her footsteps backstage, the echoing sound of her footsteps as she walked out on stage, the distinct sounds of the audience clapping, the hollow silence in the pause before she plays.

She would also *feel* herself walk on stage, bow, grasp the edge of the organ and slide onto the bench, feel the temperature of the keys, the heat of the stage lights.

The technique is to select several of these elements, and, one at a time, imagine seeing, hearing, or feeling them and immediately re-experience your outcomes. The sights, sounds, and feelings will then prompt your internal state. Connecting the anticipated sights, sounds, and feelings with you desired internal state will also keep you from entering an unpleasant state when you experience them.

Imagine the details, even though you may not be aware of them during the perrformance.

Marilyn decided to start with the feeling of her hands just before she began her warm-up, and how they became warm as she moved through her routine. As she recalled the feelings in her hands moving from cold to warm, she pulled up her outcome. The images of *giving the audience something* flooded her — the *musical slip of mind,* the *warm, unobtrusive glances of her mother, growing as an artist,* and the rest.

Next she chose the purplish glow in the greenroom, and the sight of the mirror. Again, she rehearsed seeing these cues in her mind's eye and then re-experienced all of her images of the performance. She went back and forth — seeing the mirror, seeing her outcomes, seeing the mirror, seeing her outcomes, faster and faster, until they blended and thinking of the mirror immediately brought to mind her outcomes.

She continued imagining each external sight, feeling, and sound of the performance, and associating the full, refined "vision" of her performance with each of them.

If Marilyn had not known what she would have seen, heard, or felt at the performance, as sometimes happens when performing in a strange place, she could have chosen generic sights, sounds, and feelings. Certainly there would be some kind of lighting. Certainly there would be some kind of sound to the auditorium. She could tie her state to open-ended details, such as "when I hear just what the sound on the stage sounds like, " or "when I see the way the light hits the music."

Here are some cues you may choose from:

Feeling your performance outfit coming on to your body.

Hearing the change from ambient backstage sounds to the ambient onstage sounds.

Seeing your accompanist's facial
expressions and hearing his or her
tone of voice.

Feeling the blood come to your head and
the stretch behind your legs as you
bow to the audience.

Seeing the bright light in your eyes as you
face the audience.

Seeing the different expressions on the
audience's faces.

Hearing the opening tone of the first piece
spill into the silence.

Feeling your contact with your instrument,
or feeling the sensation of singing
the notes of your pieces.

Hearing the coughing and clatter of the
audience in the periphery.

These kinds of sensory stimuli will create a mold to
pour your inner state into. Taking time to work through
every conceivable external cue and attach your outcomes
to them is the most important work you can do. It will
prevent you from singing beautifully in the shower yet
terribly on stage. It will also prevent you from seeing the
bright spotlight and unexpectedly feeling thrown off. You
will have anticipated the experience, seen the spotlight,
and it will have triggered your refined inner state and
readiness to perform. This is the step that enables you to
carry through your work into the performance.

## Summary

After we had talked for about an hour, Marilyn looked completely different. A soft shimmer seemed to pour out of her into the room.

Her dingy imagining of the performance, of herself feeling helpless, had now transformed into a composite of all of these qualities:

> *giving the audience something*
> *working passionately*
> *growing as an artist*
> *seeing her mother and teacher's nurturing glances*
> *seeing the audience getting something valuable*
> *seeing herself as a compassionate, strong, determined*
> *woman who learned from her mistakes*
> *connecting with it like people working together*
> *feeling courage and joy*
> *sensing the music emanating from the core of her being*
> *feeling firm, yet highly animated in her muscles*

She had paused her train of thoughts, ventured into herself to select and refine each one of these individual qualities, and had worked to pull them all together. She had no objections about the state it put her in. She knew she had a lot of ground to cover, but she was up for it. The idea of this performance as an opportunity to capture these qualities excited her, plugged her in. And finally, the qualities were rich and concrete and vivid. She felt them in her body. She heard it. She saw the images. They were right there, tangible in her experience, connected to all of what she would see, hear, and feel as she walked out on stage. She had done her performance work and prepared an internal condition that was conflict-free, compelling, and rich. And, with all of those qualities flooding the hall, the audience could not resist getting wrapped up in the music.

I attended the performance and the sponsor, in fact, moved around the stage in a highly distracting manner. He started to pace from one side of the organ to the other, feigning to turn pages with great importance. His walk had a distinctive, eye catching spring and occasionally the man even looked directly at the audience and smiled.

In the first few minutes of the performance, however, Marilyn made it obvious that the music was much more interesting than the sponsor. She was so committed and involved in her playing that we in the audience could not take our eyes off of her. Before long, even the sponsor became wrapped up in her performance. She did not play a flawless technical performance. Ordinarily, she said later, she would have mentally gone over and over a mistake during the rest of the performance, completely distracting herself. Instead, whenever she made a mistake, she glided over it, carrying the beauty and excitement of the music into its full bloom. At the end, Marilyn received a standing ovation with several call-backs and the reception afterward was full of warm and gracious feelings. It was a successful performance.

| Category | Description |
|---|---|
| Outcome | To at least give the audience something, even if it wasn't technically perfect. |
| Beliefs:<br>   1)about possibility<br>   2)about meaningfulness to the performer, his support group and the audience<br>   3)about identity | Possibility — working *passionately*. Meaningfulness — growing as an artist, pride of her mother and her teacher, satisfaction for the audience. Identity— woman who learned from her mistakes, glided over them. |
| Values | a sense of people working together. |
| Emotions | An emotion between courage and joy. |
| State of Mind | focusing on the music, yet not on the music...on the flow, the connection, like when the music expands. |
| Physiology | firm, yet agile and highly animated, viscous (thick) feeling. |
| Time and Place of Performance | feeling of hands warming up, purplish glow of the greenroom, creak in the door, hollow footsteps onstage, bow, audience clapping, grasping the edge of the organ and sliding onto the seat. |

Chart depicting Marilyn's work.

# V

## ARTISTIC GRIT

     As you begin to prepare your music, you can think of your upcoming performance as though it were a blank canvas. It may have a few sketches of what you want on it, or perhaps none at all. You can recall how we discussed the Action/Outcome Grid, where you attend to as broad an idea as your desires as a musician, down to as specific an idea as how to handle a phrase. You can recall the categories to choose qualities from — your beliefs, emotions, values, state of mind, and physiologies — and how to enrich your outcomes from the Action/Outcome Grid. These give you a broad palette of experiences, that, like an artist, you can use to color-in your performance with what you want, until it is rich, fully realized, and compelling to you.

An objection,
resistance, or
conflict is defined
as *anything* that
interferes with
100% commitment.

Sometimes, though, you may look toward your performance and instead of seeing a blank canvas, you may see an intense representation of what you *don't* want. A towering image of a disappointed teacher may glare in your face, or "I'm not good enough" may blast in your ear, or a heavy sinking feeling may drag in your muscles. You may feel unprepared, not up to "everyone's expectation" of your performance, or not up to the technical demands of your performance. The conductor, the audience, or even your own inner musical sensitivity may frighten you. Instead of starting with a blank canvas, your performance may already have these images colored in, shaking your confidence, weighing you down, creating unpleasantness — in essence, preventing you from achieving one hundred percent commitment.

Sometimes you may see part of what you want and part of what you don't want. You may look to your future performance and feel an intense desire for brilliant technical execution. One part of you may say "Yes, this is what I want," and at the same time another part of you may feel, "Yeah, *but* I've been through this before. I'll push myself, get tense, lose sleep, get frustrated, and go through sheer hell, because it will never be good enough — yuk!"

The object of your performance work is to resolve your conflicts, satisfy your objections. Using the above example, you will need to find a way *to achieve technical brilliance* without *going through sheer hell*. It may lead you to an unexpected perception of the performance, but once you find the solutions, the performance will fit you like a glove.

You may find, too, that when you satisfy one objection, you may get another objection, and after you satisfy it, you may get still another one. There may be six, ten, seventeen, or twenty-five objections in all, but eventually you will run out of them. It is important for you to learn to work until you run out of all of them: with no inner objections, something magical will begin to happen with your performing. The wellspring of your whole self will flow through the music and will transcend ordinary participation with your performances.

I asked my performance class, "Who in here has objections for their next performance? O.K., Gretchen. What is wrong?"

"I don't have control of my high notes," she said.

"All right, anything else?" I asked.

"No, just an uncomfortable feeling."

"No control of high notes, an uncomfortable feeling. Who else? Susan? What seems wrong with your performances?"

"I can't get down to my low notes without pushing."

"Any others? Just call them out."

"Nerves."

"No musical flow."

"Uncertain memory."

"Fear."

"Wishy-washy — sometimes I'm on, sometimes not."

"Time, too little to practice."

"Confidence (lack of)."

The class members were nodding. Gretchen leaned forward and asked, "What can we do ?"

You can *use* these kinds of experiences. In the big picture, they are simply signals that something is wrong, and your job is to keep changing whatever is wrong until it is right. Fortunately, your objections will lead you to the qualities that are right for you. And, because you will need to find what is right for you in order to reach one hundred

I become excited when I meet an objection. I know it is there because I am entering new territory, and I know that when I solve it, I will have taken one more step in my artistry.

percent commitment, your objections can be thought of as the grit that will stimulate your artistry.

The first and most basic idea about how to resolve your conflicts is this simple premise:

*Every objection has an intended benefit — its own underlying outcome — for you.*

This premise is at the heart of successfully working with yourself. Though the benefit may not always be obvious, it is always there to discover. Once you have looked behind the objection and found its benefit, you essentially have another outcome. And you can develop that outcome just we have in the previous chapters. Keeping this premise with you as you work with your tensions, fears, and anxieties will take you a long way toward resolving them.

To resolve your objections and evolve your artistry, look at the following list of steps. Like the Four Procedures to build an outcome, these too resemble points along an assembly line to move your objections through.

1) recognize the original outcome
2) recognize the objection
3) discern the objections's intended benefit
4) find a solution to satisfy the intended
    benefit of all parts
5) test the solutions
6) adjust, if necessary
7) get the outcomes to work together
    with the solutions

Let's follow along in the next story of Wilma, and stories of a few other musicians to illustrate how this basic step-by-step process can be applied. Keep in mind that even though these seven steps can become as automatic as an assembly line, every objection and personality is unique, so these steps will always be highly individual.

Wilma came into my office — a beautiful woman with a beautiful voice, an extremely talented musician. Currently, she was doing post-graduate work and taught voice at a university. She was having a difficult time feeling good about herself and her voice. Several years earlier, she had loved to sing, and took great pleasure mastering her art. She had experienced several traumas related to her voice, however, and ever since had struggled with it.

As she arranged herself comfortably at the other end of the couch, I was impressed with the richness of her personality. She already exuded an expansiveness that lit up the room. She spoke with a deep, low voice and her luminous eyes moved quietly.

Since this was the first time she had come to see me, I explained to her that we were not going to sing just yet and would instead discuss what she would like to have in performing. I asked her to describe why she wanted to perform in the first place, what qualities she would miss if she quit singing, and what was special about it — what her outcomes were.

At first she didn't speak; her eyes lost their luster and the corners of her mouth drooped down. At last all she could say was, "It is so *hard* to sing. I work so *hard*, I try so *hard*. I'm just so afraid."

I realized sadly that she was completely separated from all of what she wanted in singing. She could only answer my question with what she *didn't* want. Her sagging body and her emphasis on the word *hard* indicated that her objection was primarily a feeling. I asked her a few more questions to articulate the objection just a little more.

"Would you know what you wanted — would you enjoy singing, perhaps — if your work wasn't so hard and you weren't so fearful?"

"Well, yes, I would, I suppose. I guess. I don't

Ask: What benefit
is this objection
accomplishing for
me?

If you are struggling with
something about your
performing, ask yourself
what you were trying to
accomplish in the first
place. Then you can ask if
it is still worth it.

know. I have just got to get myself together."

"I have a hunch that the part of you that feels afraid and works hard is attempting to accomplish some benefit for you," I offered.

"Well, I don't know what it is."

"Speculate for a moment. What *could* the benefit be, supposing that there was one?"

She paused thoughtfully a moment.

"Protecting me."

"From what?" I asked

"From the unknown, from hurting myself," she said.

"*To protect you from hurting yourself* would certainly be beneficial, wouldn't you say?" I said energetically, amplifying the benefit. "I mean, how lucky to have something inside you looking out for you like that."

"Yes, but it stops me."

"From what?" I asked. The answer to this question would be another, conflicting outcome.

"Freedom to sing, try new things."

At this point, the dynamics of her conflict are clear. The objecting part is a hard feeling, mixed with fear. It wants *to protect her from hurting herself.* Even though she has a better understanding of what the hard feeling is doing for her, she is still not convinced. The other side of the conflict is an urge *to sing with freedom, to try new things.*

She needs to satisfy both sides of the conflict — the desire to feel protected (which is characterized by the hard feelings) and the desire to sing with freedom (which is characterized by trying new things).

*Recognize the original outcome*

Wilma's original outcome was *to sing with freedom.* She had completely lost sight of it because it aroused her intense hard feelings as she pursued it. The hard feelings, in fact, had grown so unpleasant that it was the only thing left about her singing.

When we discussed what *to sing with freedom* meant to her, she explained that she had sung for a famous teacher in a series of workshops. In these workshops, the teacher directed the singers to hang over, roll around, leap around the room as they sang, ostensibly to free up their singing. Instead of feeling freedom when she tried these exercises, however, Wilma felt sore, bruised, and dizzy. But, when she saw the techniques help the other students, she developed the idea that she must make them work for her too; otherwise, she concluded, she could not sing freely.

Even though Wilma was miserable, notice how fine her original outcome to *sing with freedom* is. Without this desire etched somewhere in her blank future performances, she would never become a fine singer who sings with freedom. Once she re-connected with her original desire to sing with freedom, Wilma could work with it, recapture the significance of it. Rolling around on the floor was, after all, just one way to learn to sing with freedom. She could use her objections to lead her to other techniques that suit her better. She could ask herself, "If not these techniques, what, specifically, would free my voice?" or "How else could I rehearse?"

It is important to keep sight of what you are pursuing because it is possible to lose it, as Wilma did. Your original outcome has in it the promise of the qualities you hoped to attain. By re-connecting with your original outcome, you can re-discover where you want to go and put yourself back on a track that you *can* commit to. You can find other ways to realize those qualities.

After reorienting to your original outcome, you may find that it no longer appeals to you (often a sign of artistic maturity), which only means that you are free to begin again and start with fresh, more desirable outcomes. Whether you find new ways to meet your original outcome

As a performer, you need an appreciation of your whole self, the totality of your personality, which may reach far beyond the borders of your thinking about the performance. You may only see a small part of the performance, while your objections can come from elsewhere in the overall performance. Searching out and satisfying each objection, even if it seems incomprehensible, is important because the totality of your personality— not just what you are conscious of — is what will flood the music with its quality and is what needs to become conflict-free.

or decide to abandon it and pursue others, you will no longer need to be bogged down with what you don't want.

*Recognizing the objection*

Wilma saw no reason that she should feel hard feelings. Her thinking added up this way:

*I want to be a singer with a free voice + I see other singers getting a free voice rolling around on the floor + this celebrated teacher must know what she is talking about, otherwise she wouldn't be celebrated = I must roll around on the floor and do other "new things" in order to sing freely.*

The negative consequences of jumping around on the stage and feeling dizzy ultimately expressed itself in her hard feelings. The hard feelings functioned to keep her from going through this unpleasantness. But because these consequences were not included in her thinking about how to sing with freedom, the hard feelings seemed irrelevant. She just got mad at herself for not being "as good" as the other singers. She just tried to persist through the unpleasantness until it finally wore down her spirit and drenched her with hopelessness.

Recognizing your objections is not always obvious, especially when you are caught in it. To feel hesitant, afraid, or discontent can feel mystifying and incomprehensible, especially after you have worked on everything you thought you should have, studied conscientiously, or diligently followed your teacher's instructions. Some musicians say things like, "No! I know what I want and I have no objections about having it. I just get too damn nervous and my palms sweat too much." The objections can seem to have no relation to the outcome.

Objections also express themselves in many different forms. Tension, self consciousness, lack of confidence, fear, confusion, disappointment, hopelessness, dissatisfaction, emptiness, condemnation, lapse of concentration, frustration — are all examples of objections. Objections can be intense, like stage fright, or subtle, like a desire to adjust the breath to shift the tone delicately. It can be an urge to hear the pitch ring with higher frequencies.

Sometimes there are so many objections that it is quite confusing to work with them one at a time, to keep track of them. When I work with a performer, I usually write down a simple list to keep track of them. Such a list may look like this: sweaty palms, concern for memory slip, off-balance feeling, fear of losing control, tension in upper back, confusion, intruding internal criticisms during the performance, frustration, hesitation. You may give each objection a color, or a name, like Ambitious, Angry, Creative, Intellectual. You can even imagine that each objection occupies a place within a circle. These are all effective ways to tag the objections, sort them, and keep track of them.

To reach a conflict-free inner state, it is important to recognize *all* of your objections. A marvelous and fun technique to accomplish this is the "If..., then..." technique. Its purpose is to elicit all of your objections (and your outcomes). Though simple, it is highly effective.

*If you had _____, then would you have EVERYTHING you wanted?*

To begin, express at least one quality you want in your performances. Then ask yourself "If I had that, would I have EVERYTHING?"

If the answer is no, then ask yourself what else you want. Once you have the answer, re-ask the question.

THE

PERFORMER

PREPARES

To enjoy myself

To not be tense

To have the audience
enjoy themselves

To reach an artistic peak

To feel confident

Some outcomes here are
negatively stated. That is
fine for this exercise. You
are looking for objections
and out-comes that you
may not have been aware
of. Once you get them all,
you can "tune" them.

Keep answering and re-asking the question until you no
longer have anything else to add.

For example, a cycle of questions and answers
might go like this:

> What do you want to happen in your
> performance?
> I want to enjoy myself.
> If you enjoyed yourself, then would
> you have everything you
> wanted?
> No, I'd like to not be tense.
> If you enjoyed yourself, and were not
> tense, then would you have
> everything you wanted?
> No, I'd like the audience to enjoy
> themselves too.
> If you enjoyed yourself, were not
> tense, and got the audience to
> enjoy themselves too, then would
> you have everything you
> wanted?
> No, I'd like to reach an artistic peak.
> If you enjoyed yourself, were not
> tense, got the audience to enjoy
> themselves, and reached an
> artistic peak, then would you
> have everything that you
> wanted?
> It would be close.
> What else would you add?
> Confidence.
> If you had .... and so on, until
> Yeah, that's it. That's about it.

Eventually, you will run out of qualities to add.
You may find fifteen, or twenty-five, maybe only seven.
But you will get *all of them*. Your answers will constitute
your wish list. You can write down each quality and then
develop them using the procedures for building outcomes
and the Tuning Questions discussed in Chapter 3.

Keep in mind that an objection does not rear its head until some part of the personality begins something. In Wilma's case, Wilma's objections (I try *so hard*, work *so hard*...) did not begin until she began pursuing *singing with freedom*.

The skills of negotiation come into play, because, like two people locked in a stalemate, the original outcome wants one thing and the objection wants another. The first step is to discern what benefit each is pursuing. By discovering the benefit that each part is pursuing, it becomes much more possible to negotiate satisfaction for both of them. Roger Fisher and William Ury of the Harvard Negotiation Project call this process *focusing on interests and not positions*. Dr. Grinder and Dr. Bandler call this process *separating the intention from the behavior*.

Wilma's case would look like this:

|  | Intention | Behavior |
|---|---|---|
| Original Outcome: | To sing freely | To sing while jumping around and hung over, and to try other "new things." |
| Objection: | To protect self | Feel hard feelings. Withdraw from singing. |

*After just a little brainstorming.*

|  | Intention | Behavior |
|---|---|---|
| Original Outcome: | To sing freely | Use TQ2 and ask "Sing freely how, specifically?" and refine her outcomes. Go to another teacher. Focus on technique. |
| Objection: | To protect self | Ask the other students why they didn't get dizzy. Use TQ1 and ask "Protect myself from what, specifically?" Find examples of times she has learned well choosing her own style. |

With more brainstorming, Wilma could find many more ways to accomplish her outcomes. By separating the intention from the behavior, she can now more easily discover a satisfactory solution for *singing freely* and *protecting herself* at the same time.

One simple approach to find an objection's intended benefit is to ask it directly, "What are you accomplishing for me?" Some people report success when they treat the objection with respect and say things like "I know you are accomplishing something for me, and I want to sing better, and I'm wondering if you will tell me about what you are accomplishing for me?" You can also try guessing, or pretending, and you will very likely be right on the mark.

Another way to peel away the crust of what you don't want and to get at the underlying benefit is to ask, *"What would you have if you had that?"* For example, an internal dialogue might go like this:

> "That memory slip! I am never going to humiliate myself again in performing. I am simply not going to perform!
> What would you have if you didn't humiliate yourself again?
> I wouldn't have embarrassment.
> And if you didn't have embarrassment, then what would you have?
> Peace of mind.
> And if you had peace of mind, I wonder what you would have?
> I don't know, freedom, freedom to express myself with confidence.
> And if you had that, then what would you have?
> A feeling of purpose."

peace of mind

freedom to express myself
with confidence

a feeling of purpose

This question is most useful when what you want seems to depend on someone else. It will help you put your wants within your own control. Notice how easily this question couples with the "If..., then" technique. For example:

"I want the judges to like me.
What would you have if the judges
    liked you?
Excitement, encouragement, a feeling
    of participation.
So , if you had excitement,
    encouragement, and a feeling of
    participation, regardless of
    whether the judges like you, then
    would you have everything you
    wanted?
No, I'd also like for them to not shake
    me up.
What would you have if they did not
    shake you up?
Confidence, I suppose, an ability to
    command my own feelings.
So , if you had excitement,
    encouragement, a feeling of
    participation, confidence, and the
    ability to command your own
    feelings, regardless of whether
    the judges liked you or not, then
    would you have what you
    wanted?"

This process of question and response could go on until all of the objections have been elicited.

*Satisfying each intended benefit*

Now that you have reconnected to your original outcome and discerned the intended benefit of the objection, you can satisfy each of them. You will need to do one of the following:

1) modify your original outcome to accommodate the intended benefit underlying the objection

2) add more resources to your original outcome to accomplish the objection's underlying benefit

3) change to another better outcome that you already have

**Modifying your original outcome**

Modifying your outcome is a good place to start to resolve any objection. Often, the outcome can be adjusted slightly by the objecting part itself, as though it were a consultant adding a finishing touch. For example, an internal dialogue might go like this:

"Well, I'd like to feel more
    comfortable while I'm
    performing. I get rather tense.
O.K., adjust your ideas of performing
    so that you can be comfortable in
    just the right way. Notice what
    would change."

After identifying a change, you can ask the objecting part: *"Is it as comfortable as it needs to be yet?"* If not, continue to modify your ideas of the performance until the tension is satisfied.

Sometimes an objection has several outcomes that need to be modified to work together. The following story about Shirley can illustrate what I mean.

When Shirley performed on the piano, her talent occasionally surged through her playing and produced warm, inspiring moments of intense beauty. When she felt these moments, everything merged together and her technique became extremely agile. These feelings were the payoff for studying hours every day. But, mysteriously, some part of her would cause these feelings to dry up and go away, and she would spend the rest of the performance trying to recapture them, only to end up feeling confused. When her musical feelings dried up during the performance, it devastated her.

I suggested that she speculate on the possible benefit of the drying up of her rapturous musical involvement. What might it be? What was the part of her who "dried up" her experience doing for her?

She stared blankly at me. "What do you mean? It's not doing *anything* good for me. It's ruining my life."

I asked, "What do you suppose it would get out of that?"

"Nothing."

"Nothing at all? Guess. Pretend there is a reason. What *could* it be?"

For a moment, she stared off to the side, then dropped her eyes to her lap, absently fidgeting with her watch. After a few moments, she looked up at me and said, "I don't quite understand, but a little voice inside just said, 'To keep you protected.' "

I suggested that she ask that part what it is protecting her from.

"From expecting too much," she said after a long pause. After a few more tuning questions, she discovered that when she began to feel musical she would begin to imagine performing in front of millions of people. In other words, the feeling of the music flowing through her would excite her ideas of a successful career. Her reasoning went like this: *"Since I am sounding this good, I'll really be able to perform in big places. And then I'll be respected, appreciated,*

Keep in mind that your goal as a performer is to prepare an internal state that is conflict-free. You want to resolve any part's objections so that your whole personality can commit to your performance. You do not want one part of you holding you back. Nor do you want to push against the part that is holding you back. You want to satisfy it so that it can be incorporated into your effort instead of holding you back.

A question to to ask yourself is 'What do I need to modify in order to satisfy the intended benefit of this objection?' Shirley needs to modify something to satisfy these three intended benefits.

*invited to special occasions, meet exciting people."* Without noticing it, a mental image of herself performing on a grand stage flashed across her mind the precise moment her musical juices began to flow. Not only did it interrupt her concentration, but it also started another event — a dialogue with another part of herself who believed that talent alone is not enough to build a career. That part of her did not want her to become excited just because she was talented. Then, another event: she became angry with herself for not staying concentrated. All this happened in a split second and, after a few times, caused her to "dry up."

These distinct events, however, contain within them the intended benefits of the objections:

*To become enraptured, involved in the music
(and stay involved).*

(the intended benefit of the part of her personality that initiated the beginning beautiful flow and became angry when it was interrupted)

*To achieve high standing as a performer.*

(the intended benefit of the part that flashed the picture of herself playing on the grand stage)

*To realistically evaluate what it takes to
build a career.*

(the intended benefit of the part that warned her about becoming too excited about her career)

Notice that, even though they are jumbled, these outcomes actually compliment each other. They simply need to be modified to work better together. A simple solution is to modify the timing of them and enrich her ideas of what it takes to achieve a prestigious career. To modify her timing, she imagined planning her career at times when she wasn't performing, such as when she was alone at home, or while driving in her car, or during her walks in the park. She practiced seeing the image of herself on a grand stage *only* at those times.

Then, to enrich her ideas, to become more realistic, she developed at least seven or eight images of herself doing what she believed was necessary to build a career. She included images of meeting the right people, learning the ropes of the business, and performing often in smaller halls. When she finished, she had modified the single image of herself on a prestigious stage into a series of images that progressed, like stairsteps, from the present point in her career to the final big one.

"The whole thing feels better," she said. "It feels more whole, and I can add more of what I need," she said.

"It's more appropriate, no doubt," I said, judging by the relaxed tone in her voice. "There is nothing wrong with calling up an image to strive for, it just needs to happen at the right time and it needs to be complete enough," I commented. "Your objections initiated the need to modify the image until it felt right."

Once more, she asked the part that was responsible for her "drying up" if it was now satisfied with the new series of images and whether these new changes protected her *enough* from expecting too much. A nice warm feeling and a gentle smile suggested that it was, and she no longer felt her talent "drying up" when she began to play well.

Recall for a moment the story of organist Marilyn, described in Chapter 4. Her primary objection was that she would become too distracted while the organ-concert's sponsor flitted around on the stage. She would feel scattered and unable to command her involvement in the music. As a result, she felt helpless to produce a compelling performance.

Adding more
resources

After her attempts to get the sponsor off the stage failed, her outcome became to command her own inner feelings even with him on stage. To solve this problem, she needed something else to enter the picture, a stratagem, resource, method — something *additional* to manage the situation.

She found an example from her past experiences of reading while she was on the bus, and being completely involved, even with the distractions of a group of kids, horns from the traffic, the stopping and starting of the bus. She focused her memory of being on the bus, reading in an absorbed state, as though she were there again, looking at the pages. With a little practice, she re-experienced the state where she tuned everything out. Then, while she was still in the state, she imagined being at the organ with the sponsor turning her pages. Suddenly, he didn't seem distracting to her at all.

She could have searched for other solutions, too. She might have found another way to talk to the sponsor and get him off the stage, or found some way to re-arrange the organ on stage so that he couldn't distract her. The possible solutions to her objection are numerous. She simply needed to brainstorm.

An additional resource can be an attitude, an emotion, another way of talking to yourself, a manner of seeing things in a new light, of hearing things differently. It could be anything. When you are working to resolve an objection, explore every possibility and do not censor any ideas. You can draw from your past experiences, as Marilyn did, and ask yourself "When and how did I ever handle a similar kind of experience?" Use role playing and ask yourself "Who do I know that could handle this in a way that is admirable to me? What would happen if I handled it the same way?" You can even ask yourself "What do I think would solve the situation?"

## Already having a better outcome

Richard was an ambitious young pianist who was just beginning his career. His years of self promotion, networking, and publicity were finally paying off. This year he had thirty scheduled concerts and, for the first time, his fees were enough to support himself and cover his expenses. It was his dream come true.

For the first time, too, however, he began experiencing problems with his rehearsals. With his rigorous schedule ahead of him, he neatly planned a detailed rehearsal schedule, but at his appointed rehearsal times, he found himself talking on the phone, reading the newspaper, or sightreading unrelated music.

After he explained his situation and showed me his schedule, I asked him if he had always rehearsed with such a tight schedule. I had the Action/Outcome Grid in mind — the issue levels and the rehearsal stage. Maybe he didn't think of himself as the kind of musician who had a tight rehearsal schedule, I wondered.

"No. I really haven't."

"What were they like — your effective rehearsals?" I asked.

"Well ... I'd usually do a few warm ups, then a little reading. And then I'd gradually slip into working on a section here and a section there."

"Did you ever have trouble rehearsing this way? For previous performances? I mean, did you end up unprepared at curtain time?"

"No... not really."

"I'm curious, then, what prompted you to change your rehearsing to this highly organized style?"

"I don't know," he said, perplexed. "I guess that since I have more music than ever, I thought it would be easier to learn if I planned it better."

"You wanted to learn the music easier by planning better," I echoed. "That certainly sounds reasonable. But some part of you gets interested in newspapers."

He nodded attentively.

"What would that part say, I wonder, if you asked it what it thought of your new style of rehearsing?"

A devilish grin spread across his face. I gave him a devilish grin back. I could see that he was surprised that part of his personality was so distinct, active.

"Consider this" I suggested. "You have improved to the point that you can earn a living performing by rehearsing with your old patterns. Your rehearsing has worked. Changing the way you rehearse to this dreary, over-organized method may not fit you, even as reasonable as it seems. Is there any particular reason your old rehearsal habits would not meet your schedule?"

As he explored that question, he discovered that, at the time he decided to "plan better," part of him had already conceived his rehearsal strategies in his comfortable style. In other words, he already had a developed outcome that would better prepare him. His plan was more casual (seemingly), but he could enter the kinds of states of mind that enabled him to learn faster. The detailed rehearsal schedule would actually interfere with his best working style.

To summarize, when you have a feeling that something is not quite right with your performance, you can use that feeling. It will lead you 1) to modify something about the outcome; or 2) to find other appropriate resources; or 3) to give up an outcome in favor of another, better one.

*Testing the Solutions*

The next step is to test your solutions. The best test is to try the solution in a real situation. But you can also test by imagining the situation. Imagine the performance. See the stage, the lights, hear and feel yourself make the music, only this time include your new solution. The more details you can imagine about the situation that used to trigger the objection, the better the test.

Marilyn found the example of reading on the bus to tune out her sponsor. Then she tested it by imagining being in the performance situation with the sponsor. She saw the organ, saw his face, and saw the music; she felt the organ chair, felt herself reaching for the keys, and felt the heat under her outfit as the performance wore on; and she heard the pages turn, the sound of the organ, and the click of the keys — all in her imagination. It was just as if she were there, except that this time, she was feeling the way she felt on the bus, in a state of mind that enabled her to tune the sponsor out. It worked for her.

If the solutions will not work — for example, if Marilyn had found that she was still bothered by the sponsor — cycle back to generate or select more options to satisfy the objections. Be tenacious about meeting the standard set by the objection itself. If the objection is still present after you have tested your solutions, continue your work to satisfy the objection.

### Adjusting the solution if necessary

When you test a solution, you may find that even if it doesn't satisfy the objection completely, it offers partial satisfaction. The solution may simply need to be altered slightly to reach full satisfaction.

Also, any trial test of a new solution may produce serendipitous insights into your artistry, and you may want to keep them. Even if the objection persists, keep the happy results and use them where they are appropriate, as well as continue your work to satisfy the objection.

### Getting the outcomes to work together

Once you have successfully tested your solutions, ask all of your outcomes involved if they will work together in your performance. This becomes one more check to make sure there are no more hidden objections. This step will also help lock in the change and keep the old conflicting habits from re-emerging. Also, ask the objections to agree to use the new solutions as regularly as they previously interrupted you. Wait for a signal that they will work together. If you get another objection, then recycle it through these seven steps. Of course, if the objections are not genuinely satisfied, then you will not get the results you want. If this happens, back up and work to find a better solution.

## Summary

Managing the many forms of objections and satisfying them requires brainstorming and creativity. Satisfying them all will require persistence. Even when your objections overwhelm or confuse you, and you feel as lost as a traveler in a foreign city without a map, these seven steps can rise up like signposts and lead you where you want to go.

1) recognize the original outcome
2) recognize the objection
3) discern the objection's intended benefit
4) find a solution to satisfy the intended benefit of all parts
5) test the solutions
6) adjust the solutions, if necessary
7) get the parts to agree to work together with the solutions.

Tapping into the multiplicity of your personality and getting your whole self to work as a unit for the time on stage is essential for peak performance. The deep qualities of beauty in an inspired performance come from the qualities of the whole self working together as a unit, free of conflicts. And, when you think about it, it is also a privilege to pull yourself together exquisitely. The work can be extremely rewarding.

# VI

## S T A G E
## F R I G H T

There are many different kinds of experiences that we musicians call stage fright. We each have our own interactions with stage fright. Sometimes, stage fright is an experience that actually serves us: it functions as a transition from an ordinary state into a searing, intense performance state. Without it, we would never reach our peak performance. Perhaps it could be modified, but if it functions well within our individual personalities, there really is no reason to change it.

Along these same lines, stage fright sometimes is not stage fright at all — it is just adrenaline and the performer has simply not gotten used to it. I have often helped performers simply by helping them get used to feeling the adrenaline, excitement, and richness in their bodies as they perform, even to the point of liking it. They come to appreciate the necessity of the adrenaline, the heightened intensity required of performers. Clarifying and enriching their outcomes and resolving their objections so

Performing is a heightened experience, so it is normal to feel dramatic changes in your body and thinking when you prepare to perform. It is entirely possible to learn to become comfortable with this intensity, even to refine it, harness it, direct it. This intensity is often mistaken as stage fright.

that the adrenaline is properly channeled will often take care of this kind of stage fright.

In this chapter, I am going to discuss another kind of stage fright, the kind that is debilitating. If you have this kind of stage fright, read on: I will present effective solutions in this chapter. Fortunately, even though stage fright can become unbearably intense, it can be handled easily — once you know how. We will look at two additional ideas and their related techniques that will help you eliminate the debilitation.

Let's consider an experiment that Dr. Milton Erickson performed, which can offer several insights related to stage fright. While teaching at Detroit's Wayne State University, he instructed his medical students to take their final exams in the room where they had attended classes all year. Most of the students passed and many of them scored high marks. Then, Dr. Erickson instructed them to re-take the same exam in another room. It was a room that the students had never been in. Surprisingly, few of the students scored well in the unfamiliar room.

We can speculate on how the familiar room enabled them to perform better on the test. In the familiar room, the same muffled air, the same grey carpet, the same hum of the florescent lights had accompanied the student's learning. Dr. Erickson's voice — his inflections, pauses, and tones as he presented the class material — had drifted in and out of the same muffledness, the same grey carpet, the same hum. Perhaps these associations — the environment and the information — triggered the student's memory of the class material and helped them recall the information for the test.

In the room where they had never been before, however, there was no familiar muffledness or grey carpet or hum to remind them of a past discussion. There wasn't anything in the room to stir the students' memory. Instead, the unfamiliar surroundings didn't remind them of anything needed for the test, and might have even disoriented the students.

If you suffer from stage fright, your unpleasant experiences may have begun with a similar setup: you may have stepped out of your familiar surroundings and into the unfamiliar glaring hot lights on the stage, into the unfamiliar sounds of a shuffling, coughing audience and felt disoriented. You may have found that the first sounds of your music seemed pale or suddenly unfamiliar as they disappeared into the open space. Or perhaps you felt an unfamiliar surge of adrenaline and it alarmed you, robbed you of the easy flow of your familiar musical know-how. And perhaps the necessity to keep going, to keep spitting out the demanding notes, in spite of it all, gripped you and wrenched your internal state into a full blown stage fright. Unfortunately, it only had to happen one time.

Considering the medical students of Dr. Erickson, however, you can appreciate how easy — even how probable — encountering confusion in a first performance can be. Without associating your musical learnings with what you will see, hear, or feel in the performance situation — a requisite performance skill — you could easily become disoriented. If your stage fright originated because of these circumstances, you should reconsider the matter. Rather than deciding that performing is not for you, you should give yourself the opportunity to learn this basic *skill* — rehearsing as if you were actually in the performance. You can acquire this skill by both deliberately associating your learnings with the sights, sounds, and feelings of the performance, as we discussed in Chapter 4, and by performing more often, which will give you more opportunities to assimilate your experiences.

The second concept about stage fright is that it is like a bad habit. Some psychologists call it a stimulus-response pattern. Dr. Genie LaBourde calls it a learned response to a given stimulus. The stimulus can be an external cue, like the sight of an audience, or an internal cue, like a mental picture that intensifies and looms over the performer, even at just the thought of performing.

The overall pattern is that whenever the stimulus enters the performer's perception, it automatically triggers the intense fear. The solution to this kind of stage fright is to break the stimulus-response — the habit of feeling intense fear at the stimulus — and then substitute other, more appropriate feelings.

Working alone to solve this kind of stage fright may be tricky because you can slip into your phobic response as you try to resolve it, and, once you are experiencing the phobic response, you are really not capable of changing it. So before any effective work can begin, you will need to separate yourself from the unpleasantness, get yourself comfortable, and keep yourself comfortable as you work. Though solving stage fright is possible to do alone, as described in the following exercise, you may want to work with a professional.

The following step-by-step procedures are highly effective. Though they may seem like silly mind-games, they have successfully helped many, many musicians comfortably perform in auditions, concerts, and recitals that at one time made them shake with terror, and after applying these techniques, perform as gracefully as if they had done it all their lives.

The following exercise is designed to create another stimulus-response pattern. The first task is to ensure that you stay comfortable. Find a strong comforting feeling and touch yourself in a unique spot in a unique way. For example, just as you feel the comforting feelings, touch yourself on the wrist, squeeze a finger, or draw an invisible line on your forearm. Or touch yourself and immediately feel the strong, pleasant feelings. Practice associating the comfortable feeling with the distinct touch until the touch automatically triggers the comfortable feeling. Then, later in the exercise, should you begin to feel unpleasantness, you can re-stimulate the comfortable feelings.

Timing the touch so that it corresponds to the feeling can resemble patting yourself on the head while trying to rub your stomach. You may get the good feeling and then lose it while you remember to touch yourself, or vice-versa. With a little practice, however, you will be able to coordinate the two.

Do not proceed until you are able to feel the strong comforting feeling with your touch. You will be successful overcoming your stage fright only when you can stay separate from the intense feelings. Having this bail-out touch to trigger a strong comforting feeling will come in handy, should you begin to feel the phobic response.

Next, imagine that you are sitting in a theater. Make sure you are comfortable. You can use your trigger touch to reinforce feeling comfortable.

Next imagine floating up out of yourself, up into the balcony, so that now you can see yourself sitting comfortably in the theater and you can see the blank stage further away. Do not proceed until you are able to see yourself sitting comfortably in the theater.

Next, read through the rest of the exercise and then perform the instructions very fast.

Looking from the balcony, at all times, watch yourself sitting comfortably in the theater. See the you in the audience watch a still image of you up on the stage just before you become afraid. There should be three separate representations of you: one in the balcony, where you are comfortably sitting and watching everything else, one sitting comfortably in the theater, and one on the stage, not yet having a phobic response. Then, as you stay in the balcony, still comfortable — use your special trigger touch at any time — still looking at yourself sitting comfortably in the theater, watch yourself on the stage go through the phobic response in black and white, all the way to the end, until it is over and the you on the stage is through feeling phobic. Then stop the scene as though it were a still image.

Next, while the scene is frozen, slip back into yourself in the audience, and then step inside the you up on the stage, in the black and white still shot of you *after* you have gone through the phobia. Now there should only be one representation of you and you are looking through your eyes.

Once inside, turn the scene to brilliant color and run it backwards, so that everything moves backwards, from the viewpoint of looking through your eyes. Go very fast. Take only a couple of seconds. You should feel what it would feel like being in a movie of yourself becoming phobic, running in reverse, at high speed, *from the inside.*

This technique, bizarre as it may seem, will usually break the habit of feeling phobic. You can repeat it several times, if you need to.

Variation

After you feel comfortable sitting in your imaginary theater, instruct the creative part of you to float up into the balcony. While you remain comfortable — again use your trigger at any point that you may feel uncomfortable — ask your creative part to replay an edited version of your becoming afraid on the stage. Like a director, it can add different soundtracks, different voices, or different pictures. It can become like watching a Monty Python-like series of images. Or it can run the scenes in black and white, make them move three times as fast as usual, or in reverse, or in different colors. It can turn scenes of yourself becoming afraid into still images, like a slide projector show, or as though it were happening under a strobe light. It can make the images smaller, or so big, that, like a giant's stage, you cannot see what is happening.

Throughout this entire editing/directing show, it is important to stay comfortable, sitting there watching yourself go through all these feelings. If you get any unpleasant feelings, try your trigger touch. If it doesn't work, stop. Success in this exercise depends on your separating from the unpleasant feelings and remaining comfortable.

Have the creative part of you keep editing until the entire phobic response is gone.

Either one or both of these techniques are highly effective. They can usually handle the worst stage fright imaginable. This same technique, for example, is currently being used to successfully treat as severe a stimulus-response problem as the post-traumatic stress syndrome disorder suffered by some Vietnam veterans. These procedures can work for you when you need to face a large audience or a special auditioning jury.

It is important to realize that the term *stage fright* is applied to many different kinds of experiences. It may refer to an objection and have an important underlying benefit for you, an outcome you need to pay attention to and satisfy. It may function to heighten your performance experience. It may just be adrenaline you need to become used to. It may just be a habit of feeling intense fear, a stimulus response, which can be broken using the techniques in this chapter. Or it may be a combination of all of these. Use the Tuning Questions, the four procedures for building your outcomes, the seven steps to resolving objections, and the techniques described in this chapter to tune your inner state from an undesired fear to one that enables you to fulfill your deepest desires.

# VII

## CONNECTING WITH THE AUDIENCE

Pat's disposition was soft, feminine, and charming. She had a lovely speaking voice and a delicate laugh. She told me that she had terrible stage fright and that it was worse performing in front of a judge.

"Really?" I inquired. "What happens to give you stage fright?"

"What do you mean?"

"How do you think of the audience? What do you see that is so scary?"

"Ohhh," she said. "They bother me."

Her eyes opened wide and her head recoiled backward, suggesting that she imagined the audience getting very large, very fast. I asked her about it.

"I know this is an unusual question, but when you think of the audience, how do you see them. Are they small or large?"

Her eyes widened again. "They are *large*," she said. "And *close*," she added.

"And how about yourself. Are you large too?"

"No. No, I am not," she said softly.

Pat was not unusual. Many performers perceive the audience as larger than themselves (sometimes as giants with bulging eyes) bearing down on their tiny selves on stage. It is not surprising that they feel under a microscope, overwhelmed: in their imaginations, they *are*.

"Let me tell you about a young tennis player," I said to Pat. "It will give you an insight into performing without that kind of fear. After he had beaten Jimmy Connors, a sportscaster asked him 'How do you play with such command of the court. Weren't you nervous or intimidated to play against Jimmy Connors?' This young tennis player paused a moment and remarked insightfully, 'No...Not really. When I view my opponent, he seems to shrink. It is as though I become very tall, huge, and when I hit the ball towards the little man in the little space on the other side of the net, I feel powerful, free — like I can move any way I want to.'"

"What an unusual comment," I said. "Yet it is easy to imagine how he would feel in command of his match. By imagining himself that large, he could feel that his racket could reach anywhere on the court. He could probably even imagine touching his opponent on the head with his racket.

"On the other hand," I added, "you can imagine how rattled he would feel if he felt small, and thought of the court as huge and his opponent as huge, leaning down on him."

Pat was nodding her head.

"Like the tennis player, musicians need to command themselves in front of an audience. In fact, performers who command the stage view their performance much like this young tennis player: in utter command of themselves and their surroundings. It is part of their perception.

She stared past me. It looked as though she was already experimenting with these ideas. I asked her about it.

"Can you imagine being larger, as large as, say, the ceiling? And being on stage, in front of the audience? What is it like?"

"It's different... It's really different."

"O.K. Let's back up and do this a little more thoroughly, now that you have had a taste. We need to add a very important step, which will not only give you a feeling of commanding the stage, but also of connecting with the audience. First, tell me what you love about performing. What attracts you to this music?" I wanted to get her outcomes.

"A nurturing feeling."

"Elaborate on what a *nurturing feeling* means," I requested.

"It's hard to describe. It's almost as though the audience transcends themselves and surrounds me, sharing in the music."

The timbre in her voice became distinct and poignant as she spoke. I was impressed with how richly she had developed this state.

"Good. Keep feeling that special quality," I instructed. "Feel it everywhere, all over you. And as you continue to feel it, imagine being on stage, growing larger. Become as tall as 6 feet...10 feet... as tall as the ceiling. Feel the nurturing quality grow with you, and even spill out of you, pour into the hall, and into the audience. Feel the essence of that nurturing quality envelope the hall, touch the audience all over..."

She was beaming.

"...and when the audience and the stage are completely saturated with that special nurturing quality,

## Work with well defined outcomes

It is important to begin this exercise only with well developed outcomes. By the significant change in Pat's expression, I knew that her experience of her outcome, her 'nurturing feeling' was extremely refined and developed. Otherwise, we would have developed it before proceding.

Like all of the
exercises in this
book, this one is
best done and then
forgotten. The
concepts will form
into an integrated
whole, and you will
not need to think of
them consciously.

*switch* views and see yourself through the eyes of an audience member — see yourself on stage, tall, flowing with those nurturing qualities, and feel what it feels like being that audience member, feeling those nurturing feelings coming from the stage. See and feel everything about it, for as long as you need to."

After a few moments, I asked her what the exercise did for her.

"The *whole* performance makes sense somehow..."

She looked very much at ease. With this simple exercise, she had given herself another description of her performance. Instead of seeing an overpowering audience snuffing her out, she saw herself, the performance, and the audience as a single, manageable expression, full of the qualities that deeply attracted her, and poised easily within her grasp. No doubt, her perception of her performance was now much more useful.

This simple adjustment in perception is the basis of a "commanding the stage" and a "connecting with the audience" quality. I had always heard that these qualities were inborn and could not be taught. Yet I've seen performers begin to shine with these qualities after applying this exercise.

Some musicians are familiar with this perception, but had never thought to apply it to performing. Shirley, for example, said that she prepared to teach her junior high choir class by seeing herself towering over her unruly class. She added that she must prepare herself this way: otherwise, her kids would run over her. It was an easy step for her now to prepare for performing this way. You, too, may have areas where you command yourself and those around you. Like Shirley, you can borrow from them and bring them into your performing.

Like Pat, when I ask performers about it, they usually are not aware of how they conceive of the audience and themselves. But once we explore their perception, we find that usually timid performers have a concept where the audience, or judge, is much more powerful than they are and that usually performers who command the stage have a concept where they are powerful relative to the audience. This second concept is so often present with performers who command the stage, and so often absent from those that don't, that I have come to think of it as a basic performance skill.

After talking with many musicians and trying different ways to teach the skill, the basic technique for acquiring these qualities is composed of four distinct steps. For convenience, I call it the Switcher Technique.

1) Step into the time and place of the performance when you are fully involved in the qualities you desire.

2) Intensify the experience of those qualities, usually by becoming larger.

3) With your imagination, involve the audience in your intensified experience, usually by seeing them surrounded with it.

4) At the height of the intensity, switch views and see yourself through an audience members eyes.

Keep in mind that there are many variations on how to apply this technique. You should experiment with it by following the basic pattern. But then, like riding a bike, after you learn to coordinate a few basics, you will get the hang of it and can then elaborate on it. You will also begin to hear other musicians describe this experience. For example, Beverly Sills said that she has always prided herself on being able to see herself clearly on the stage. Her comment presupposes that she imagines herself through the eyes of an audience member and has an idea of how she will appear to the audience. Performing as beautifully as she did, you can reasonably guess that she saw herself performing admirably. Switching positions, no doubt, also helped her quickly see different approaches, to evaluate what would and wouldn't work.

Also keep in mind that, like riding a bike, this skill is best understood when you do it. The first few times you work with it, it may surprise you and offer a treasure chest of interesting insights and desires for performing. Each of these desires can then be re-worked, clarified, intensified, and brought into the act of performing.

*1) Step into the time and place of the performance when you feel fully involved in the qualities you desire.*

This step assumes that you are already in touch with what you want (and that any objections have been solved). You can begin with a single quality, as I did with Pat and her desire for a *nurturing feeling,* or you can combine several qualities, and begin with them all.

The most important consideration of this step is that you *experience* the quality you desire while you imagine being on stage, in front of your audience. If you have a special feeling of beauty, then put yourself into that experience. Feel it in your muscles. See it in your imagination, hear it in your inner hearing. This step begins where the exercise in Chapter 4 of associating the qualities with the time and place ends: it begins by imagining being on stage, experiencing all of your desired outcomes.

*2) Intensify the experience of those qualities, usually by becoming larger.*

Though most people feel their desired experience intensify when they imagine becoming larger, some people do not. For them, to imagine becoming larger only makes them feel awkward. The most important consideration is to somehow work your imagination so that you and the qualities you desire are "larger than life," so that the qualities exceed the magnitude of the audience.

Start with becoming larger. If that doesn't work, cycle through each sense and adjust it. For example, if you see an image of what you want, see it become clearer, more saturated with color, more three-dimensional. If what you desire is a sound, hear it as more stereophonic, louder, clearer, more resonant. If it is a feeling, imagine it moving all over your skin, all over the floor. Imagine tapping your foot and sending a tremble of this special feeling under the chairs and feet of the audience.

Metaphors can also help, such as thinking of the audience as though they were in a doll house, and that they were special and at your concert to feel special.

It is also extremely useful to imagine the quality even exceeding yourself. A visual representation might pour out of your skin; a feeling might smooth out the air around you; a sound in your inner hearing might echo outside of yourself. Each of these, of course, would represent the epitome of your most attracted-to values, the ultimate expression of what you want in performing, the essence of what you utterly identify with and feel conflict-free about. If the qualities you are working with are not that attractive to you, then you will need to back up through the previous exercises to get to this point.

*3) With your imagination, involve the audience in your intensified experience, usually by seeing them surrounded with it.*

The important consideration here is to make sure your imagination includes the audience, that they are not isolated from the qualities you want. Again you can cycle

Pianists, for example, can imagine a feeling in their finger, then imagine the key becoming larger and full of that feeling. Then they can imagine the strings full of that feeling. Finally they can imagine the finger-key-string connection becoming larger and more full of those highly desired qualities.

through your senses. You can see your chosen qualities, as colors, or sparkles, or crystal clear ideas, flow over and around the audience, behind their chairs, in their ears — everywhere. If it is a touch, imagine reaching over and touching the audience members. Get your exquisite feeling on *their* skin, or imagine it penetrating *their* inner feeling. If it is sound, imagine the quality penetrating *their* inner hearing. You can imagine that every sound you produce, even when pianissimo, comes pouring out of a super-sensitive stereo system with speakers lining the walls, under the chairs of the audience, from directly above, flooding the hall with the most transparent and rich tones imaginable. You want to saturate the audience and the hall with what is so special to you about performing.

*4) At the height of the intensity, switch views and see yourself through an audience member's eyes.*

This is the step that connects you with the audience. Re-experience all that you have just built up from the inside of an audience member. See what they would see, this huge crystal clear, vibrant color — whatever it is. Feel what you would feel with all of that special quality from the stage touching you. Hear in your inner hearing the richness of those qualities flowing into your hearing from the stage. Experience this position for as long as you need to.

You can get the point of view of several audience members, even other performers on stage. You can step back into yourself on the stage, and feel again what it is like. Each time will yield something more for you.

### Summary

This exercise is very effective in moving yourself toward commanding your performances and connecting with the audience. Like everything else, it needs to happen in your imagination before it will happen on stage. Every performer will perceive the audience somehow: envisioning them as overpowering will yield one result; envisioning yourself as full of what you care about most and touching the audience with it will lead to another, better result.

Cheryl, a fine student, summed up the exercise with a particularly elegant observation. She said that, prior to the exercise, she had always thought of the audience as people she had to conquer (she was complaining of feeling scattered, of too much energy on stage). Now, however, she could relax a lot more, work with the finesse of her artistry, because she could now imagine how the audience would benefit from her performance. "It is like a wall has come down that was between me and the audience."

# VIII

## GETTING IT
## ALL TOGETHER

The following transcript illustrates how the ideas in this book could be applied in a session. This transcript taken from a master class held at Texas Woman's University, March 1989. The singer is Betty Wintle, a professor of voice at Southeastern Oklahoma State University. Her accompanist is Dede Benton.

(Betty sings 'Quando m'en vo soletta' from <u>La</u> <u>Boheme)</u>

Robert: You have a big, beautiful voice, so you have a lot of good things that you can bring to your performance. One of the ways to start to find out those things is to figure out what you want in a performance. So, I'm coming up to you and I'm saying, "Gee, Betty, I would love to be able to sing, but I don't really know why I would want to sing. What's so special about singing?"

Betty has just seen me work with a singer and so knows some of the kinds of questions I will ask her. I begin by orienting her to her outcomes.

*Betty begins to describe some of what she wants: the audience understanding, enhancing the music, have an expressive voice. She says these matter of factly, so I ask for more. I want her to find what makes her light up.*

**Betty:** Well, trying to make the audience understand what you're singing about in a way that enhances the music and the poetry. And maybe your voice can be expressive with the emotions.

**Robert:** But, Betty, why would I want to do that? I don't really —

Betty finds her first real outcome, *Fun.*

**Betty:** Because it is fun.

**Robert:** Because it's fun.

*Doing it well.*

**Betty:** When you do it well... When you don't do it well, it just makes you ...

*If...then* question to get all of her outcomes. I keep asking her for what else she wants until we get a full list . You will hear me try to repeat them all to keep track of them. In your own work, you can write them down.

**Robert:** So if I did it well, then I could have fun with it and that would be why I would want to do it?

**Betty:** That would be one of the reasons.

**Robert:** O.K., what's another one?

*To express the music, feel the music.*

**Betty:** Well, I have something in me that makes me want to express music, makes me feel music.

**Robert:** O.K., what is that?

*To share expressing the music.*

**Betty:** And I want to share that.

**Robert:** So what is that like, to share something?

*To feel exhilaration.*

**Betty:** Well, it's kind of exhilarating when you are *really* sharing it.

Robert:    Oh, when you are *really* sharing it.

Betty:     But in order to share something, you have to have someone who wants it.

Robert:    You have to have someone who wants it.

Betty:     Yeah... who wants you to give it to them. You want them to be receptive to it. And they won't be if you don't do it well.

Robert:    They won't be if you don't do it well. So, if you do it well, then you can have fun, and you can share this thing in you that gives you this sense of exhilaration and they'll be receptive. And if you have all that? What else, is that all of it?

Betty:     Probably not.

Robert:    O.K. Now, that sense of exhilaration seems like a lot of fun. And about their being receptive and doing it well, how would I know when I did it well?

Betty:     When it was *easy*.

Robert:    When it was *easy*.

Betty:     When it was easy and you felt like it was all very expansive and it just sort of engulfed whatever you were trying to portray.

Robert:    So if it was easy and expansive. Then I could have fun in that sense of exhilaration.

At this point, it may seem that Betty's outcomes depend on someone else — a receptive audience. However, as she clarifies what she means, her outcomes are actually dependant upon herself and whether she *does it well*.

*If...then* question.

*To sing easily.*

*Easy and expansive.*

*If...then* question.

*Energy.*

Betty: And the energy.

Robert: The energy.

Betty: The energy that helps give you the breath.

*If...then* question.

I try to match her words as she states her outcomes. This helps me help Betty by not imposing my own interpretation on what she means.

Robert: Because then if you had the breath you could do it well. Have that sense of expansion and that easiness, and then what would I have? Fun?

Betty: You'd have fun.

Robert: O.K.

*Shimmer.*

Betty: But there also has to be a shimmer in it.

*TQ 4*

Robert: A shimmer. O.K. What would happen if there wasn't a shimmer in it?

Betty: It would be dull.

Robert: It would be dull.

Betty: And boring.

Robert: And boring. O.K. How would I know when I had a shimmer in there?

Betty: When you had that energy and excitement that engulfed the room.

Robert: So, I wouldn't have to worry about whether I

had the shimmer or not, as long as I had that energy and excitement engulfing the room.

Betty: Right, it would just be there.

Robert: It would just be there because of the enhancement. Would you have any objections to having any of that?

Betty: Not a bit.

Robert: Have you had it a whole lot? I mean, do you have it often?

Betty: Fairly often.

Robert: O.K. Often enough?

Betty: No.

Robert: When you don't have it, what happens?

Betty: Well, you mean what causes me not to have it?

Robert: Yes.

Betty: Being nervous.

Robert: O.K. being nervous. So, if you weren't nervous would you have it more often?

Betty: Yes.

At this point, we have all of her outcomes — *fun, doing it well, to express and feel the music, share expressing the music, sing easily and expansively, to feel exhilaration, energy, shimmer in her voice.* If she had all these qualities, she would really get what she wanted. Now we move to step 2: What interferes with her having it? And what do we need to do to solve those objections?

An objection, *being nervous.*

I want to know how she gets nervous, what she means by it.

**Robert:** So if I were you and I were going to get nervous, how would I get nervous? What would I have to do? I can walk up here and look around the room...

**Betty:** By thinking more of what the audience thinks or thinking that there is something wrong...worrying about whether or not it's going to be right, whether or not the breath and energy are going to be there.

**Robert:** O.K. Now if I were to worry about that, how would I be worrying about that? Would I be talking to myself going "I don't know if that's right, you gotta watch your breath" Is that what would be going on?

**Betty:** Yes. You might see someone's face and start thinking maybe the person isn't looking like they are enjoying it, and you start thinking about that rather than what you're doing.

I am testing to make sure this is the right objection to her outcomes *If...then* question.

**Robert:** If I were to get nervous so I didn't have that exhilaration and that free-flowing expansiveness and that something in me to share and then the fun that comes that brings the shimmer in the voice, would it happen because I saw someone's face and then started worrying about what they were thinking?

She is beginning to discern the real interruption to her outcomes.

**Betty:** That would happen, but I think maybe the reason for all that would be not concentrating on the positive things hard enough to begin with.

**Robert:** Not concentrating on them hard enough to begin with.

Betty:     Or consistently enough.

Robert:   Consistently enough.

Betty:     Yes, because when the concentration stops, then
           you notice other things.

Robert:   When the concentration stops, and it stops when
           you see someone's face or it changes when you       *TQ 4*
           see the face. Well, I'm wondering what would
           happen if when you look at the face you didn't
           discuss what they might be thinking.?

Betty:     Well, that happens sometimes, and I just go on
           singing, and it's fine.

Robert:   If I'm singing and you're teaching me how to
           sing exactly like you do, the good times and the
           not-so-good times — and gosh, I sure do want to
           do this right — I have to know when to start
           talking to myself, right?

Betty:     I would say, "don't talk to yourself!"

Robert:   Yes, but if I'm going to do it exactly like you, I'd
           have to know when to do it and when not to do
           it. It's not just arbitrary.

Betty:     Well, I think I do better if I don't talk to myself.

Robert:   Right, but when you do, when it interrupts, I
           would have to know when to make sure I
           interrupted myself.

Betty utters the
intended benefit of
the interruption — *to
get a really sparkling
tone.*

I am emphasizing the
intended benefit.

| | |
|---|---|
| Betty: | Oh. |
| Robert: | I mean, I'm looking one time and I don't talk to myself, but another time I do. What's different? What do I have to see that's different about looking out there? |
| Betty: | I'm not sure, it has something to do with worrying about whether the tone is really sparkling. |
| Robert: | Now if I were to worry —, |
| Betty: | Silly, isn't it? |
| Robert: | No, it's not silly at all as a matter of fact, my hunch is that the part that is worrying about the tone reaching the audience and the shimmer and having enough energy and all the things that you worry about is doing something for you. In other words, it kicks in every now and then, almost like, "hey, let's make sure that tone's good." Well, I mean, how much does a singer need a part like that? Just a little bit, or a lot? I mean, suppose you're a singer and you didn't have a part of you that really wanted to make sure you sang with a beautiful tone? What kind of singer would you be without a part like that? |
| Betty: | Well, kind of haphazard, I guess. |
| Robert: | O.K., but this is no haphazard part of your performance personality, it's pretty dedicated to, *committed* to helping you have a good tone. |

Now, sometimes, it doesn't always help you get a good tone. It gets you worried about what they're thinking and then you get nervous and you lose the exhilaration and so on, right?

But, it's *committed* still to helping you have that, right? So, I'm wondering if that part that brings in the worrying, if it would have any objection to trying some new way to make sure you had that tone without interrupting.

Betty: I think it *would* like to have some other way to do that.

Robert: O.K.

Betty: Because I don't think it *wants* to interrupt.

Robert: O.K. So, is there any other part of you that would give it what it needs? In other words, how else might you have a good tone? Besides, the way that it's doing.

Betty: I think there is a *courageous* part of me that has this strong backbone — and —

Robert: Well, have *it* show you how to have a good tone!

Betty: And when I do that this other part doesn't usually get in the way.

We are beginning the process of meeting all of her outcomes, especially the part of her that interrupts.

Betty's tone suddenly becomes strong as she says this.

Betty is adding a resource to meet her objection.

<table>
<tr>
<td>As I speak, Betty is putting it together. Her expressions shifts subtly.</td>
<td>Robert:</td>
<td>O.K., so ask that courageous part if it could work with that part so the two of them together, the courageous part and this interrupting part, can give you that good tone. And you know about having a good tone. O.K. How's that working? Any objections to that? (Betty shakes her head) None?</td>
</tr>
<tr>
<td>Testing the solution.</td>
<td></td>
<td>O.K., now is it possible to have that sense of exhilaration, and that sense of sharing, and the expressiveness while these are working that way?</td>
</tr>
<tr>
<td></td>
<td>Betty:</td>
<td>There's more calm.</td>
</tr>
<tr>
<td></td>
<td>Robert:</td>
<td>More calm. O.K. It feels that way, right?</td>
</tr>
<tr>
<td></td>
<td>Betty:</td>
<td>Umhum.</td>
</tr>
<tr>
<td></td>
<td>Robert:</td>
<td>O.K., any objections to having that feeling?</td>
</tr>
<tr>
<td></td>
<td>Betty:</td>
<td>No.</td>
</tr>
<tr>
<td>Locking-in the solution.</td>
<td>Robert:</td>
<td>Will you have this part and that courageous part take responsibility for making sure they give you both of those while you are singing, especially since there are no objections to it? (pause) No objections?</td>
</tr>
<tr>
<td></td>
<td>Betty:</td>
<td>No.</td>
</tr>
<tr>
<td></td>
<td>Robert:</td>
<td>O.K., it looks pretty good then. Feels good.</td>
</tr>
<tr>
<td></td>
<td>Betty:</td>
<td>Yes it does.</td>
</tr>
</table>

| | | |
|---|---|---|
| Robert: | Now, any objections to having that exhilaration feeling, I mean if you are looking out and you see that face and it looks that particular way, can you imagine talking to yourself? And interrupting yourself? | More testing. |
| Betty: | No. | |
| Robert: | O.K. So, if I — | |
| Betty: | Am I supposed to? | |
| Robert: | No! I didn't think you could. | |
| Betty: | I can't. | The solution works so well, she cannot even get the interruption. It surprises Betty. |
| Robert: | And that's better for singing, isn't it? | |
| Betty: | Yes. | |
| Robert: | O.K., now, let's go to that *exhilaration feeling*. Because it comes from back here, it comes out, doesn't it? | Now we want to get all of her outcomes together. |
| Betty: | Yes. | |
| Robert: | O.K., now you know what that feels like, and it's a very special feeling. Right? And you know what that *fun* is like? You know what that *shimmer* and that *expansiveness* and that *energy* is like? Right? Now, what I want you to do is let your imagination take all that and bring it all together for you until all of them are there. They're all there? O.K. Any objections to that? Is | |

there anything you would like to add to make it even better?

Betty: I don't think so. It seems to me that I was always trying to get rid of this part and now you have turned it around so it is actually helping.

Robert: Yes, any objection to that?

Betty: No. I like it.

Robert: In fact, you can have all of your parts working together. Did you know that *that* is part of performing ... getting every single part of you committed to performing? It's kind of a simple idea, isn't it?

Betty: Yes.

Robert: How can you perform with only half of you?

Betty: It's not easy.

Robert: Just bringing out a little part to perform... It doesn't work that way. So, we bring all of our parts and we get them until there are no objections. Makes sense, doesn't it? It's a simple idea, of course. Then your muscles can relax, because when conflicting ideas put tensions in you like that, then you can't sing that way, right?

Betty: Right.

Robert: O.K. So, now you have this idea of that *energy*. You know what it's like.

Betty: Yes.

Robert: And I'm wondering what you can do to make that energy even better.

Betty: Make it more expansive, more and more confident. Singing to the whole world instead of the whole room.

Robert: Imagine that, singing to the whole world instead of the whole room. O.K., any objections to that?

Betty: No.

Robert: None.

Betty: I have to get a little bigger than I thought for that.

Robert: Go ahead and get as big as you need to get.(pause) Is that big enough?

Betty: I think so.

Robert: O.K., now I want you to try something that's a little bit different. Now as the picture gets bigger, and you step into it, what I want you to do is let the picture get bigger, but more full of those qualities, and as you step into it, feel the feelings get as big as that picture is. There you go, now how's that? Any objections?

Now that we have the qualities that she desires all together, and have her objections to them satisfactorily solved, we begin the next step — *enrich them.* By the way, at this point, Betty's appearance is becoming more attractive. She is feeling very much at ease in front of the audience.

Betty needs just a little bit of guidance on building intensity. She responds beautifully.

Betty is literally beaming.

Beginning the *switcher* technique, described in Chapter 7.

Betty rehearses mentally, only in her imagination. It gives her a chance to put it all together *before* she sings.

Betty:     No.

Robert:    Stay in that picture while it is that big with those feelings being that big and in the middle of it, open up and see even a larger picture with you having that fun and that excitement, and step inside it and let the feelings get as large as that one... There you go. And now again, open up and see it even bigger. And now this time step inside it and let the feelings get that big. Now, any objections to that?

Betty:     No.

Robert:    It's kind of nice, isn't it? Now you know what I want you to do? I want you to stay in that feeling that big, and while it's that big, I want the feeling itself to go out to all the people in the audience, in other words, I want you to move and when you move, the feeling just spills out of you. The feeling itself gets bigger. And imagine it going all around the people. It can go all around here, and around there, and as you look all around, imagine it there and at the peak of it, *switch* and look back at yourself, large with those special feelings. How's that feel? Feels different?

Betty:     Yes.

Robert:    Now, notice what it's like to imagine singing full of this feeling at this size. Hear the opening of the song with all these feelings. You may need to work it in together. That's right. Now bring in more of that big feeling. Now see the first phrase, you can see that phrase, can't you?

When you see that first phrase, I want you to feel this feeling until seeing the first phrase and feeling this real large feeling is one and the same thing. Yeah, there it goes, now that's the work we're after. That's right, now go to the next phrase, and as it begins, you have this big feeling. That's right. Any objections?

Betty:    No.

Robert:   O.K. Now go to the next phrase. Any objections?

Betty:    No.

Robert:   Now go ahead and try it this time and as you really do it, notice what it's like to really feel that big feeling.

(Betty sings)

A beautiful rich voice pours into the room.

Robert:   O.K. how's that?

Betty:    I liked it. It was fun!

Robert:   Different?

Betty:    Yes, thank you so much.

Robert:   Well, we can take it a little further. Any objections to that?

Betty:    No, as long as we have the time.

We are at a new level, one that might bring up new wants. We can start the process over — find what she wants, clear any objections, and build it into a rich experience while she is singing.

Robert:   Was it different over here?

(audience cheers)

Dede (the accompanist): Oh, it was wonderful! You had about three times the voice.

Robert:   How about that? Did you have more of that kind of —

Betty:   Yes, I wasn't worrying, I was just being and doing.

Robert:   Yes, with the freedom of just being and doing. What could you add to make it even better? Now, see it's one thing... you're here and you make one thing change, and 'Ah!' It's better, but you know —

Betty:   I know it's not as good as it can be, but I'm not sure exactly what needs to go into it.

Robert:   What needs to go into it. Well, let's play around with this, because once you get over one hurdle... You know, you're an artist. You're saying "O.K. Now I've got to build this performance. I'm no longer nervous. I no longer look at the audience and talk to myself. I've got my parts working together. I've got it nice, it's a nice performance. *But now I'm going to make it better.* " Now, as you evolve as an artist, with whatever you choose to make it better, you're now more able to do it and draw things in — once you develop that skill. So the question is "What is it that I could bring in to it? What are the kinds of qualities that could come from... " guess where?

From you. From inside of you there are all kinds of things you can add to your performance to make it better. And you can experiment, can't you? So, if you were going to add something, a particular quality, what do you think it would be?

Betty:     I'm not sure, unless it would be more expansiveness.

Robert:   Let's try it.

Betty:     I feel that it could be bigger, more energetic... *I* could be bigger, and even *more* energetic. I liked the feeling of the way I felt, but I feel I could do even more.

Robert:   Let's work that.

Betty:     Maybe more depths of emotion.

Robert:   More depth of emotion.

Betty:     I'm not sure...

Robert:   O.K., but it's something. You have some sense, some *something*, but you're not sure what it is that would make what it was even better.

Betty:     Yes.

Robert:  Now what I'd like you to do is have that sense, or *whatever* it is that you're not sure of, just add — without your even knowing what it is — to that whole quality.

(Dede, the accompanist, thought the pause was a cue to continue and began to play. Though Betty wasn't quite ready, she sings anyway. )

Robert:  How was that?

Betty:  I don't know, was that better, or not better?

(audience): I thought it was even more.

Betty:  Did you?

Robert:  Now what we want to do —

Betty:  I wasn't sure if I was adding the right —

Robert:  That's all right, what we want to do is do it before we sing, and what you do is you just experiment with it.

So this time I want you to take that big feeling — it's hard to do while you're singing —

Betty:  I lost a little of the picture —

Robert:  That's right, now what I want you to do is take the picture until you get all of what it was. You have any objections to that? O.K. is it all the way back, yet?

Betty's concern about how she did is a typical response when she was trying to do too many things at once. We simply needed her to reorient to her outcomes.

Betty:   I think I need to get that backbone of courage before I start it.

Robert:   Yes. This is very important. It's important for you to know that performing is *preparing* yourself. You are the main instrument of this whole thing— the performance. Then the voice and the song will follow. But first it's got to start with you. So right now, you can undo that last performance —you know how to do that, and you can already be here again. Now, you can see again that courage. You can see it all the way?

Betty:   Yes, I can see it.

Robert:   Well, how about that exhilaration?

Betty:   It's there.

Robert:   The fun, the sharing... O.K. Now, it was that other little special something, maybe, depth of emotion, some kind of —

Betty is back on track.

Betty:   I think it's a little spark that floats along on the top.

Betty identifies a new outcome.

Robert:   *Yeah.* Well, let that little spark float along. Is it there?

Betty:   Yes.

Robert:   Now, is that enough of a spark? Is it floating along?

Another outcome.

Betty:   Yes, I can see it from the whole earth.

Robert:  Yes, you can see it from the whole earth. Now, is there anything else besides the little spark that you could add.

Betty:   Maybe some pretty, warm colors.

Robert:  Add those pretty, warm colors. Aha! Any objections to that? Now, keep those warm feelings and that spark there and notice what it's like to begin, not yet actually, but in your mind's eye. Imagine singing with those qualities that way. Any objections?

Betty:   No.

Pulling the outcomes
into the singing.

Robert:  Imagine the feeling ... as you are singing... being fully integrated with those warm qualities and the little spark floating up there and the size of the exhilaration... and the fun... and the shimmer. There you go. Any objections to having them all together?

Betty:   No.

Robert:  O.K., now go ahead and sing the first part again, and this time notice what it's like to bring this into the actual feelings, those big feelings you had while you sing with this quality.

(Betty sings. It was beautiful, easy, fluid. She seemed totally at ease.)

Robert:     Now, how's that?

Betty:      I like it.

Robert:     You like it. I want to do one more thing. This is
            more of an interpretation of that sort of thing. I
            want you to take the image that's up there, and I
            want you to bring it down so that when you see
            the chairs, I want you to let this image glow
            through. Now, I only want the fullest image, the
            full warm feelings glowing through. I want you
            to see them and then see the image fully and
            then go back and then I want you to see the
            image down here. The spark floating up in that
            size... and then down right under your feet. In
            fact, I want you to even imagine seeing it behind
            you. And all over your back... and even
            including Dede... and the back window so that
            the image spreads all the way around you. And I
            want you to look around, I want you to look
            over there and see it glowing through. The
            spark... the fun... and the exhilaration... and
            seeing the camera... and the spark...and the
            exhilaration...and I want you to look and see the
            chairs and the little shine on the chairs, and
            when you see that shine, let that warmth glow
            through. It's different now, it's filling out the
            place where you are with those qualities. Now, is
            it everywhere?

Betty:      Yes.

Robert:     If you look over there do you see it? (Betty nods)
            If you look over there? If you look at your feet? If
            you look to your left side? If you were to see
            behind you? All the way behind you, Dede in

Saturating the time and
place of the performance
with her desired qualities.

Truly a beautiful per-
formance. The whole
performance, including
the difficult high note in
the aria, poured out with
an exciting, fluid ease.

the picture? When you see Dede it glows right
through?

Betty:     Yes.

Robert:    And in the sounds of the piano? O.K. Feel better?
           Feels more locked in?

Betty:     Yes.

Robert:    O.K. Now, sing it with that. And you can look at
           the audience and you can look everywhere.

(Betty sings the last time.)

Robert:    How's that?

Betty:     I liked it fine!

# IX

# E VOLVING AS AN ARTIST

Every exercise in this book is geared toward helping you prepare yourself for a performance. I have defined your readiness to perform as a state where your attitude is conflict-free, rich, and compelling. This broad definition can work for your musical style, your technical level, and your stage of development as an artist – whatever they are.

I like this definition because it can fit so many individual expressions. I am always amazed when I work with a performer to discover the qualities that excite him or her about performing. The combinations are always unique. Look at the following lists. They read almost like recipes for a performance.

* George is a performer
who has not yet been
mentioned in this book.
His list is just an
example of how unique
a performer's desires
can be. You can almost
anticipate the unique
quality of the
performance just by
looking at the
distinctness of these
three lists of desires.
Each performer will
have a corresponding
meaning of these words

| Marilyn | Betty Wintle | George * |
|---|---|---|
| to give the audience something | fun | willingness to explore |
| work passionately | doing it well | voracity |
| grow as an artist | sharing the music | courage |
| feel pride of mother and teacher | sing easily | take charge of life |
| ensure satisfaction for audience | sing expansively | celebrating, probing the beauty of the human spirit |
| learn from her mistakes | feel exhilaration | clarity of knowledge |
| sense of people working together | feel energy | essence of form, efficiency |
| feel courage and joy | hear shimmer in voice | freedom of truth, self expression |
| focus on music, feel sense of | sparkle | essence of wanting to know, refined curiosity |
| | warm, rich colors | intensity of vision |
| | | inner conviction |

I always do whatever I can to help the musician slip into their individual qualities — like those listed above — and bring them into the performance. Like magic, the stiltedness in the music will tend to disappear and a sparkle will take its place. The technical execution almost always becomes easier. The absorption into the music becomes more profound. All these qualities bring the performer directly to the edge of his or her excellence.

Then, after compiling these qualities and successfully infusing the performance with them, the performer will want something else. His new list of qualities may not be defined yet. It may sit in his imagination like a sketch. The old qualities may not be interesting to him anymore. His current vision may have flaws in it, offer new conflicts. Where he used to have a technical problem, he no longer has; instead, he has a new desire that he can't quite pull into his performance.

And he will work to develop those desires and pull them all together and find himself again with a new set of understandings about music and himself. All of the variables I have mentioned in the book will change with his experiences. He will change his values, his identity, his physiology, his outcomes as he grows older and encounters new experiences. Teachers and colleagues will offer new insights into the various facets of performing. He will learn new qualities, think of possibilities he had not yet conceived. And they will all change within him at different rates.

His artistry will evolve because his whole life is evolving. His craft of performing will be the skill of pulling these evolving qualities together for the time and place of each performance.

It might be nice to define a perfect performance — Mozart should be played *this* way, or Bach should be sung *that* way — and assume that just by matching it you will give a brilliant performance. Though there is nothing wrong with matching an established criterion, I think there is simply more to beautiful performing. Besides, our perception of the music changes through time and what seems so significant in one epoch is scorned in another. Mozart should be played non-legato in this epoch, legato in that epoch. What one teacher says is a must, another one disagrees with. When it comes to performance, there are no rules that are fixed in stone.

Unfortunately, I have known many young musicians who pursue "getting it right" and chase these elusive rules in order to improve their performances. Perhaps such a performer feels "safe" with this approach. Yet somehow, even with exceptionally fine rules guiding the performance work, without the performer fully committing himself to his performance, we in the audience miss something. We can observe that performer and observe that he or she is doing it "right" — the tempo, the style, the notes are all executed properly — but there is nothing to touch us, nothing to lead us to a new experience.

There is also a prevalent idea, especially among classical pedagogues, that the performer needs to get himself out of the way of the performance and let the composer speak though. Sometimes, this idea describes the performer as the servant of the composer. These ideas may seem contrary to the ideas presented in this book.

However, they actually fit well together. Using the techniques in this book, I would ask such a pedagogue about the quality he is pursuing from being a servant of the music. What special qualities emerge from "getting out of the way?" His answer will be some vision, some highly valued quality — a quality of freedom, perhaps — or even an individual *list* of qualities. And then I'd suggest that he develop those qualities until they are rich, compelling, and can saturate his work on stage with it.

Catherine, a piano teacher, after reading the first few sections of this book, offered her feedback. She said, "You know how much I love your ideas. And they make a lot of sense to me. But, I know some artists who do not fit into your ideas."

"Who?" I asked.

"Martha Argerich, for example. She is a sell-out for every concert she gives. And she doesn't have to work hard on everything."

"When she performs, does she seem like the kind of performer who knows what she wants?" I asked.

"Yes?"

"Does she seem to perform with an inner struggle about what she wants?"

"No."

"Do her ideas seemed drab, or well-formed and rich?"

"Rich. She is mesmerizing."

"Then, how does she not fit into what I've suggested in this book?" I asked curiously.

"Well, she doesn't have to work at it. She is a natural."

"I am not sure how you formed the idea that if someone achieves a beautiful performance naturally and efficiently that they are not working, Catherine. But consider this: If you organize yourself to perform without any interruptions, your performances will become natural and efficient, too. Martha Argerich has taken the parts of herself and organized them in such a way that she *can* commit one hundred percent. Martha is a performer who has discovered how to prepare herself efficiently. She is a skilled performer. If she doesn't spend her time laboring over and over passages like some students, the interesting question is how does she spend her time, what does she work on and pay attention to. I bet you'll find that she uses her objections, develops rich states of mind, conceives of the music in potent ways — all so that she can pull it together on stage."

I don't know any two people with the same wants, perceptions, and skills, so the material every performer has to work with is unique. Enriching the best of what you as an individual have to work with and pulling it all together is what will make you a skilled performer.

I heard another striking comment. One of my colleagues offered that he had had in his entire life only two occasions where he felt that he had completely involved himself into his performance. Both times were tremendous experiences, where he felt powerful, transcendent, where he burned with an intense fire, like a demon. He realized the significance of that state of mind, but felt helpless about reproducing it. These states were mysteries for why they came and went, and why they did not appear again.

Our conversation, unfortunately, was interrupted. I wanted to say that he could re-tap into those states of mind. I wanted to point out that during those states, something about him was tuned up just right. He can draw upon those experiences, once they are no longer conceived of as mysteries that happened without cause for his regular work. If instead of thinking of them as mysteries, he wondered about the specific way he arranged his inner condition prior to it happening — what he saw, felt, and heard — and cleared away any objections to fully transporting himself back into that experience — then he could skillfully recall those experiences and associate them with his current performing — just like Marilyn, the organist, when she recalled reading on the bus and brought it into her performing. If he devoted his attention and imagination to tapping into this state and treated this work as though it were a skill — a fundamental performer's skill — he will find many more ways to experience those states, certainly more than twice in a full career. And, by setting his outcomes, he can have those experiences in his performing more than twice in a career.

So, all these ideas boil down to a single concept — the art of performance is the art of pulling yourself together for the time on stage. It all begins with you, so you might as well pay attention to what you want, your objections, and what you need to solve them. You might as well approach the subject with an attitude of skill, rather than talent. You will accomplish more.

Your performances will work when you develop what you *want* in the music. Your desires will include states of mind, emotions, attitudes, skill acquisition, career achievements. And they will evolve, and you will need to develop your new desires.

Your performances will work when you resolve your conflicts. Your inner conflicts will develop from within your own attitudes, desires, and outcomes, as well as from the outside conditions placed on your performances. And new conflicts will emerge that will also need to be resolved.

And, finally, your performances will work when your inner state is rich. Like an artist learning to distinguish one hundred and fifty shades of orange in a sunset, rather than just two or three, you will learn to distinguish qualities in your inner experience — your outcomes, beliefs, values, emotions, states of mind, and physiologies. Your inner experiences will change and the new and richer, more refined ones will need to be re-built.

Like paintings of an artist, you will leave a legacy of your performances, all with their unique styles, and content. The ideas and techniques in this book have been described as tools so that, like brushes, you can re-use them over and over, to bring in the qualities you deeply desire. They were written for you to achieve a tuned-up state for each of your performances, to use with finesse as you progress through your artistic journey. Bon Voyage.

# APPENDIX I
# OUTLINE OF
# TECHNIQUES

The premise for the techniques presented in this book is that your performance begins in your imagination. Rather than follow a vague admonition "be more creative," this book discusses several practical techniques to develop your imagination so that it is in line with your personality. The techniques are all designed to stimulate your imagination in specific ways — and always in the direction of what you want, what is conflict free, and what is rich.

This appendix lists the techniques and questions in an easy reference form, and offers a few comments for getting it all to work together. When you are preparing for a performance, turn to this appendix and ask yourself each of the questions.

The overall concept is to develop a complete idea of the performance by orienting yourself to all of your outcomes. The next step is to refine those outcomes, support them, and resolve any conflicts that pop up about them. The next step is to intensify the concept and associate it with the time and place of the performance. Then, the final step is to forget about them, give yourself time to digest them all.

# The Action / Outcome Grid

The Action/Outcome Grid is the place to begin forming the kinds of questions you should be asking yourself. The main purpose of the grid is to stimulate you to work out every aspect of your performance.

1. Pick an *issue level* from the left-side column and a *stage of the performance* from the top row.

2. Combine the two chosen ideas with the what, where, when, how, why words to generate questions. Not every question will be immediately applicable, but you want to ask as many questions in as many different ways as you can.

3. Make a note of your answer. See the images, feel the feelings, hear what you would say. You might want to write your answer down.

4. Go to the next intersection and repeat until you have covered all intersections.

Example

Pick *technique* and *rehearsing*. Ask yourself *"How* do I want to *rehearse* my *technique?"* *"What technique (or technical problem) do I want to rehearse?"*

Comments

The Action/Outcome Grid is a tool to help prompt you to find all of your concerns. A performance is a complex undertaking and each concern will fit on the grid somewhere, so it will help you organize it all.

Some thriving businesses, such as Toyota when designing a new car, use similar brainstorming techniques. Their creative designers, engineers, sales people coop themselves in a room and literally cover the walls with 5X9 cards that have a specific concern/outcome written or drawn on them. They brainstorm, review, re-brainstorm until they arrive at a complete representation of what will satisfy all of the concerns/outcomes. The result it a well-built automobile.

## Four Procedures to Build an Outcome

These four steps can be applied to nearly any artistic urge, desire, or fundamental goal and will help you develop each one into something compelling.

1. *Make sure your outcome is stated in the positive.*

2. *Specify your outcome with what, when, where, how, and why questions.*

3. *See, hear, and feel at least five representations of your outcome. Cut and paste the representations until they are all part of the same idea.*

4. *Co-ordinate this outcome with your other outcomes.*

Comments

These steps should become second nature to you. They will discipline you to develop your ideas, insights, artistry. They also give you a specific endpoint when working you imagination: you will know you have completed your work when you have imagined at least 15 different representations of your outcome (5 in each main sense).

As you run your ideas through these steps, you will no doubt uncover other outcomes. You can cycle these new outcomes through these procedures also.

It is also important to keep in mind that you are building distinctions about what you want in your performances. The result will always be a richer concept, a more refined understanding. These steps are simply deliberate techniques to build distinctions about what you want. How many distinctions are too many, how rich is too rich? In performing music, I don't think there is an image that can become too full of distinctions, too rich, too refined. Developing your art is a lifetime committed to grinding out the distinctions in your personal, artistic vision, anyway, so go to it directly. You might as well spend an afternoon or two working your imagination with these four steps.

## Tuning Questions

These are handy questions for quickly moving your ideas along towards maturity. Like any and all of these questions, you can ask them at any point in your work.

TQ1 is for nouns. Ask 'What _____ (noun). specifically?'

TQ2 is for verbs. Ask '_____(verb) how, specifically?'

TQ3 is for generalizations. Ask (with emphasis) 'Always?' 'Forever?' 'Everybody?'

TQ4 is for can't, should, must, have to words. Ask, 'What would happen if I did (or didn't)?' or 'What prevents me?'

TQ5 is for comparisons. Ask 'According to whom?' or 'According to what standard?'

Comments

With the Four Procedures and the Tuning Questions you can tickle your imagination extremely well. These are rigorous questions to ask yourself and they lead you on the trail of connections that shape your understanding, your artistic vision.

I have often heard *"They* think this or *they* won't like that" or "I *can't* do that" from musicians when thinking of performing for judges or someone special. In this context, these questions are ever more important: "*Who*, specifically, will think *what* specifically? *How* will they think that? *How* do you know they will think that? What will happen if you did play that way?" Very often, these questions can become great liberators of your talent. You should use them frequently.

# Qualities to Support Your Outcome

Use these questions once you have an outcome.

Possibility
    Is it possible for me or someone like me in a
    similar situation to achieve this outcome?

Meaningfulness
    How would it be personally meaningful for me or
    someone like me in a similar situation to achieve
    this outcome?

Sometimes thinking
of another person
similar to you makes
it easier to imagine.

    How would or could it be meaningful to the
    people closest to me or someone like me in a
    similar situation to achieve this outcome?

    How would or could it be meaningful to the
    audience for me or someone like me in a similar
    situation to achieve this outcome?

Identity
    What kind of person could and would perform
    with this outcome?

    When was I like that kind of person, at least
    partway?

Values
    What are three different values I enjoy seeing,
    feeling, or hearing about?

Emotions
    What emotion would best support this outcome?

    (If I feel _____ in preparing this outcome,
    how would it affect my behavior?)

State of Mind
    Which state of mind will best support my
    outcomes? When were the last three times I was
    in that state of mind?

Physiology
> What body state or physiology would best
> support my outcome?

Time and Place
> What will I see, hear, and feel that will specify the
> time and place of my internal state?

Comments
This technique has three parts.
1) stimulate the search for the quality (asking the question)
2) turn the answer into a full experience (not just a word)
3) associate all of the answers (as experiences) together

The tricky part is step 2 — turning the answers into
experiences. It is easy, for example, to answer "Is my
outcome possible?" with the word "Yes." But you need to
go beyond just the word and get the image, or the feeling,
or what you say to yourself that lets you know that it is
possible. For example, you may see a picture of yourself
doing your outcome, and because you see the picture, you
know it is possible. The picture is what you want to
associate with the other answers.

Mastering step 3, associating the answers together,
is not difficult, but it does take practice. The easiest pattern
is to experience one quality (mentally seeing the image of
your doing the outcome, for example) and then
simultaneously experience another quality — with the
objective of experiencing them at the same time.
Sometimes it is necessary to go back and forth between
answers, starting slowly, and gradually speeding up until
they join together. For example, if two of your answers are
a picture of you achieving your outcome (possibility) and
a feeling of joy (emotion), then you first want to see the
image as clearly as possible. Then, as you continue to see
the image, begin to remember feeling joy. Work to bring
the feelings of joy fully into your experience, but keep
seeing the image clearly. Within a few seconds, you will
see the image and feel joy at the same time.

1) recognize the original outcome
2) recognize the objection
3) discern its intended benefit
4) find a solution to satisfy the intended benefit of the objection
5) test the solutions
6) adjust, if necessary
7) get the outcomes to work together with the solutions

Step 4 will require that you either modify your outcome, add more resources, or shift to a better outcome you already have. Use these three questions to stimulate finding a solution.

What would happen if the _____ (the resisting part) modified your outcome, adjusted it until it looked right, sounded right, and felt right? What would your outcome be like then?

Ask the _____ (resisting part) if it has another better outcome for you and if it does, have it show it to you in full detail, so that you get a full representation of that other outcome.

Ask the _____ (resisting part) to tell you what you need in order to accomplish the outcome that you don't yet have.

Comments

The trickiest part of resolving an objection is to recognize the objection and then to do something with it. It is easy simply to feel frustrated. To kick out of the frustration and begin resolving it requires practice. I have known musicians who have lived with basic conflicts for over twenty years, even though it only took two or three minutes to resolve.

# APPENDIX II

Charisma, Performance Fire, Commanding the Stage —
Talent ... or Skill?

**The Performer Prepares: Master Class with Robert Caldwell**
Video Cassette 39.95
ISBN: 1-877761-27-3

    In this companion video, Mr. Caldwell demonstrates how performance can be enhanced using the techniques from The Performer Prepares. You will see a back to back comparison of the first and last performance of singer Betty Wintle as she sings "Quando m'en vo" from La Boheme. You will see the subtle differences emerge in the performance, those qualities that are difficult to put your finger on, but you know make a better performance. The performer, Betty Wintle, becomes more relaxed, more involved, more focused — more of some intangible quality we recognize as performance excellence.

    Following the before-and-after comparison, you will see the work Robert Caldwell leads Ms. Wintle through. You will hear the kinds of questions that loosen Ms. Wintle's artistry, free her technique, and create a sparkle in her performance. You will appreciate how skillfully asking the right questions and working the performer's imagination can heighten the final performance.

    The annotated transcript of this video tape is published in Chapter 8, Getting it All Together, from this book. Each video tape costs 39.95. Add 2.25 for shipping and handling. Specify VHS or Beta format. Send check to

Pst. Inc.
Attn. Order Department
P.O. Box 800208
Dallas, Tx 75380

Or call toll-free **800-284-7043**. Ask for the ordering deparment directly.

# Order Form

Pst...Inc
P.O. Box 800208C
Dallas, Texas 75380-0208
Telephone 1-800-284-7043

Please send me the following books.

| | | |
|---|---|---|
| _____ | The Performer Prepares | @ 16.95 each |
| _____ | The Performer Prepares VideoTape | @ 39.95 each |
| _____ | Diction for Singers: A concise reference for English, Italian, Latin, German, French, and Spanish pronunciation | @ 29.95 each |
| _____ | The International Phonetic Alphabet for Singers | @ 18.95 each |
| _____ | The MusiKeys Sightreading Primer | @ 5.95 each |

I understand that I may return any book for a full refund if not satisfied.


Name _____

Address _____

City _____ Zip _____

Texans please add 8% tax

Shipping: 2.25 for the first book and .50 for each additional book.
_____I can't wait 3-4 weeks for Book Rate. Here is $3.00 per book for air mail.

_____Please send me a Performers Bookshelf brochure.